PELICAN BOOKS

Lateral Thinking for Management

Edward de Bono was born in Malta and after his initial education at St Edward's College, Malta, and the Royal University of Malta, where he obtained a degree in medicine, he proceeded as a Rhodes Scholar to Christ Church, Oxford, where he gained an honours degree in psychology and physiology and then a D.Phil. in medicine. He also holds a Ph.D. from Cambridge. He has had faculty appointments at the universities of Oxford, London, Cambridge and Harvard.

Dr de Bono is the founder and director of the Cognitive Research Trust in Cambridge (founded 1969) and the Centre for the Study of Thinking. He runs what is now the largest curriculum programme in the world for the direct teaching of thinking in schools. Dr de Bono's instruction in thinking has been sought by many of the leading corporations such as IBM, Shell, Unilever, ICI, Du Pont and many others. He has been invited to lecture extensively throughout the world.

He has written many books which have been translated into nineteen languages. He has also completed two TV series 'The Greatest Thinkers' for WDR, Germany, and 'De Bono's Course in Thinking' for the BBC. Dr de Bono is the originator of the term 'lateral thinking' and also the inventor of the classic L-game which is said to be the simplest real game ever invented.

His books include *The Use of Lateral Thinking* (1967), *The Five-Day Course in Thinking* (1968), *The Mechanism of Mind* (1969), *Lateral Thinking* (1970), *The Dog-Exercising Machine* (1970), *Technology Today* (1971), *Practical Thinking* (1971), *Po: Beyond Yes and No* (1972), *Children Solve Problems* (1972), *Eureka!: An Illustrated History of Inventions from the Wheel to the Computer* (1974), *Teaching Thinking* (1976), *The Greatest Thinkers* (1976), *Wordpower* (1977), *The Happiness Purpose* (1977), *Opportunities: A Handbook of Business Opportunity Search* (1978), *Future Positive* (1979), *Atlas of Management Thinking* (1981), and *De Bono's Course in Thinking* (1982). Many of these have been published in Penguin. Dr de Bono has also contributed to many journals, including the *Lancet* and *Clinical Science*. He is married and has two sons.

Edward de Bono

Lateral Thinking
for Management

A Handbook

PENGUIN BOOKS

Penguin Books Ltd, Harmondsworth, Middlesex, England
Viking Penguin Inc., 40 West 23rd Street, New York, New York 10010, U.S.A.
Penguin Books Australia Ltd, Ringwood, Victoria, Australia
Penguin Books Canada Ltd, 2801 John Street, Markham, Ontario, Canada L3R 1B4
Penguin Books (N.Z.) Ltd, 182-190 Wairau Road, Auckland 10, New Zealand

First published by McGraw-Hill Book Company (UK) Ltd 1971
Published in Pelican Books 1982
Reprinted 1983, 1984

Made and printed in Great Britain by
Richard Clay (The Chaucer Press) Ltd, Bungay, Suffolk
Set in Times

Contents

Preface

Waiting for creativity

Man owes his success to his creativity. No one doubts the need for it. It is most useful in good times and essential in bad. But how can one achieve it? We always admire it but complain about its elusiveness. It is regarded as a magic gift, a divine flash of inspiration, a chance coming together of extraordinary circumstances. It seems that one can do nothing about creativity except await it passively. It usually does come about in this passive manner—but only because we have never developed the type of thinking that encourages it. Creativity is a "lateral" type of thinking and it has been difficult to develop because, in many ways, it is contrary to the traditional habits of logical thinking which we find so useful. For instance, in traditional logical thinking it is necessary to be right at each step but in lateral thinking this is not important.

Active creativity

The first step is to understand the processes involved in creativity. The second step is to escape from attitudes which inhibit these processes and to use methods for encouraging them. This is the purpose of lateral thinking, which can be learned as a skill and then used in a deliberate manner in order to achieve creativity.

The nature of mind

The huge effectiveness of mind arises directly from the way it organizes information into patterns. The more firmly a pattern is established the more useful it becomes. But creativity involves breaking out of established patterns in order to look at things in a different way. Thus the very effectiveness of mind in establishing fixed patterns makes creativity very difficult. It is like having a filing system set up to store data in a particular way. In order to pursue cross-references in such a filing system, one would have to develop new ways of using it.

Basic part of thinking

Creativity is not a separate part of thinking. It is not a luxury to be used by artists. Creativity is so basic a part of thinking that it comes into every possible field: information systems, communications, financial departments, marketing, advertising and promotion, labor relations, operations research and problem solving, planning, design, research and development, public relations, et cetera. It is a bad mistake to suppose—as many do—that creativity is concerned only with new product development.

Data, ideas, and information

Ideas are the spectacles through which we look at data in order to see information. Data is useless until we look at it through an idea—only then does it become useful information. Different people looking at the same data will derive different information from it according to the idea which each of them uses to look at the data. Old data looked at through a new idea gives new information. Creativity is concerned with bringing about new ideas and updating old ones. Since data is usually available to *everyone*, it is the creativity with which an individual can look at the data that makes the big difference. Creativity is the competitive tool that matters most. Even apart from competition, creativity is necessary to develop new ideas that make the fullest use of available data.

Leap ahead

Creativity allows one to leap ahead to new ideas which themselves direct the search for more data. Ideas are more likely to generate data than data is to generate ideas. Without creativity one creeps along far behind experience; with creativity one pushes ahead of it.

Escape

Creativity is not only concerned with *generating new ideas* but with *escaping from old ones*. Continuity is the reason for the survival of most ideas, not a repeated assessment of their value. Such continuity can trap one into gross inefficiency. Freed from the prison of an obsolescent idea, one can move

2

ahead. Furthermore, ideas (like organizations) which develop slowly over a period of time tend to be cumbersome. With creative restructuring, one can slice through the inefficiency and put things together in a much simpler and more effective manner.

Practical creativity

This book is about practical creativity through the development of skill in lateral thinking. An understanding of the creative process is based on the way the mind handles information. The achievement of creativity involves: an attitude of mind, an escape from traditional thinking habits, specific formats and techniques, and the use of a new functional word. All these combine to give the skill of lateral thinking. This skill can be learned, practiced, and used. With practice and confidence lateral thinking can become so natural a part of thinking that no special effort is required.

Everyone can be creative

When creativity is regarded as a magic gift, there is nothing that can be done about it if you are not lucky enough to have the gift. But everyone can develop some skill in lateral thinking and those who develop most skill will be most creative.

Lateral and vertical thinking

Difference between lateral and vertical thinking

Vertical thinking is traditional logical thinking. It is called vertical thinking because you proceed directly from one state of information to another state. It is like building a tower by placing one stone firmly on top of the preceding stone; or like digging a hole by making deeper the hole you already have. One of the characteristic features of vertical thinking is continuity. One of the characteristic features of lateral thinking is discontinuity. This and other points of difference are considered in this section.

Education concerns itself almost exclusively with vertical thinking. This is the type of thinking that is used all the time. To many people it is the *only* possible type of thinking. It was the type of thinking that was developed by the ancient Greeks, and we sometimes pride ourselves that we have done nothing to change or improve it. Because vertical thinking is so well known and so well established, one can give a clear idea of the nature of lateral thinking by showing how it differs from vertical thinking. Unless one appreciates this fundamental difference, it is quite impossible to use lateral thinking. Indeed, many of the advantages of lateral thinking depend on the ability to escape from the rules of vertical thinking.

Some of the principles of lateral thinking directly contradict some of the traditional principles of vertical thinking. Because of this contradiction one needs to have a clear idea of the nature of lateral and vertical thinking in order to separate the two. If one cannot separate the two, then there is much confusion and it is impossible to use either effectively.

Although the principles of vertical and lateral thinking are quite distinct, the *end result* is not. By looking at a solution, it is quite impossible to tell whether it has been reached by vertical or lateral thinking. You can only tell this if you have an actual record of the thought processes involved. Once a solution has been reached by lateral thinking, it is always possible to see how that solution could have been reached by vertical thinking. For the same reason, what may be a brilliant lateral jump to one person may be a simple vertical progression to another.

A stick has two ends. The ends are quite distinct. But each point along the stick is related to both ends. The point may be in the middle or nearer one end than the other. Lateral and vertical thinking are two opposite poles but there is a spectrum between them. Any particular mental step may fall somewhere along that spectrum. It may be pure lateral thinking or pure vertical thinking, but it is usually something in between.

Many people are much concerned about whether a particular idea is an example of lateral or vertical thinking. Apart from the difficulty of deciding this once the idea has come about, it simply does not matter what you call it. In practice, the processes are usually intermingled. Nevertheless, the two types of thinking are quite distinct in nature.

First- and second-stage thinking

Most people are aware of the second stage of thinking. The first stage is taken for granted and often assumed not to be there at all. The second stage is concerned with techniques of logic and mathematics. A computer is a second-stage thinking device. The first-stage thinking ends when the data and the program have been fed into the computer. Logical and mathematical techniques are never applied directly to a situation. They can only be applied when that situation has been divided into concepts, features, factors, effects, and other perceptual parcels. These perceptual parcels are not themselves created by the application of any special techniques, but by the natural patterning processes of mind with all their limitations and arbitrariness. We assume that these starting concepts are correct, and only pay attention to the validity of the second-stage algorithms which we use to process the concepts and arrive at a "proved" solution. In other words, we assume that thinking only starts at the second stage.

It is in the first stage of thinking that the concepts and perceptual parcels are put together. We are beginning to realize that most of the trouble with our thinking results from our inability to do anything about this first stage. We have very good techniques for the second stage of thinking and we are improving them all the time. But we have no techniques at all for the first stage. Paradoxically, it is the very excellence of the computer as a second-stage thinking device that has emphasized the importance of the first stage. It is the questions that are asked of the computer and the choice of data that is fed in that determine the usefulness and relevance of the output, not the excellence of the computer processing which we can now take for granted. No amount of excellence in the processing can, however, make up for deficiencies in the first stage. In closed mathematical systems, like getting a man to the moon or solving set problems, we can make good use of computers. But in open-ended problems and in situations where the whole problem is to *define* the problem, we can do little unless we get better at first-stage thinking.

It is not only a matter of what concepts we use but also of what values we give to them. By simply changing values without changing concepts, one can arrive at very different conclusions. Even more than concepts, values are the product of the natural perceptual patterning of mind. Choice of attention area, choice of entry point, choice of factors, these are all part of the first stage of thinking. And such choices will predetermine the final result of the thinking process.

Mathematics can get to work once we have chosen to look at things in a certain way. But mathematics cannot itself choose the way we are going to look at things.

For example, there are many ways in which one could approach the problem of absenteeism in industry. One could simply measure the man-hours lost or one could measure any change in the man-hours lost. One could measure the number of men out at any one time and note whether this was a steady number or whether there were any fluctuations. One could try to find out whether the same men were involved or whether absenteeism was evenly spread among all the men. One could try to see whether the absenteeism was predictable at certain times of the year. These are all questions set up in the first stage of thinking. It would be possible to measure everything in sight and then generate the questions, but this approach becomes impossible because the number of things which can be measured and related can quickly become huge. For instance, in addition to the mere counting of man-hours one might want to see whether there was any way of telling which men were more likely to absent themselves. Or one might want to know what the cause of absenteeism was (illness, domestic organization, sports, and so on). Someone else might come along with a completely different approach, and instead of measuring man-hours lost he would want to know whether absenteeism did in fact affect production instead of *assuming* that it must do so. If it did not affect production, was this because there was overmanning anyway? Another person might turn up with a new concept of "stretching." This would mean the willingness or ability of work-mates to work a little harder for a short period of time to cover the absence of a fellow worker. Having generated such a concept, one might be able to do something positive with it—perhaps even by allowing a margin of absenteeism as part of "job satisfaction." It is clear that the mere counting of man-hours lost or the carrying out of mathematical correlations is only part of the process.

It is often assumed that it does not matter where you start in considering a problem because, if your second stage processing techniques are correct, you will eventually reach the right answer. This is just not so. If you start off with certain concepts (for example, that absenteeism is an industrial crime and is bad for production), then you may never reach the right answer. This assumption that it does not matter where you start is responsible for many well-worked-out and supported errors. In fact, the solidity of the second-stage processing only worsens the error in first-stage patterning by giving it a spurious validity.

In the first stage of thinking, the emphasis is not on the manipulation of concepts but on the concepts themselves. This is the conceptual stage and one forms and re-forms concepts, cuts across them, introduces new concepts, and so on.

There are times when the sheer availability of second-stage processing techniques is an actual disadvantage. If one cannot easily find a suitable processing technique, then one has to spend far more time looking over the approach to the problem. But if a processing technique is obvious, then one settles for the first approach that comes to mind and moves ahead with the second-stage processing at once.

Consider the following simple problem. In a singles knock-out tennis tournament, there are 111 entrants. What is the minimum number of matches that must be played? It is easy enough to start at the beginning and to work out how many first-round matches there must be and how many byes. But this takes much time. Yet in an audience of 100 people, there may not be anyone who tries a different approach. This different approach involves a change in the first stage of thinking. Instead of considering the players trying to win, consider the losers after they have lost. There is one winner and 110 losers. Each loser can only lose once. So there must be 110 matches. Had there been no other standard way of working out the matches, then this unusual approach might have been used more often, but the sheer availability of techniques leads one away too quickly from the first stage of thinking.

Skilled use of lateral thinking in the first stage can make things very much easier in the second stage. Far from detracting from the effectiveness of vertical thinking and second-stage processing, lateral thinking magnifies their usefulness, just as a gun is more effective the better it is aimed.

Lateral thinking changes. Vertical thinking chooses

Lateral thinking is generative. There is change for the sake of change. The purpose of lateral thinking is movement— movement from one concept to another, from one way of looking at things to another. Lateral thinking recognizes no adequate solution but always tries to find a better one. Lateral thinking works with the hope that a better pattern can be arrived at by restructuring. Lateral thinking is never an attempt to *prove* anything but only to explore and to generate ideas.

Vertical thinking is selective. It seeks to judge. It seeks to prove and establish points or relationships. Where lateral thinking is concerned with change and movement, vertical thinking is concerned with stability—with finding an answer so satisfactory that one can rest with it. Vertical thinking is looking for answers, whereas lateral thinking is looking for questions.

Vertical thinking says: "This is the best way of looking at things; this is the right way of looking at things." Lateral thinking says: "Let us try to generate other ways of looking at things; let us change this way of looking at things."

Vertical thinking judges what is right and concentrates on it. Lateral thinking seeks alternatives. *To laterate* indicates this sideways movement for alternatives. Laterate and lateration replace *concentrate* and *concentration*.

Vertical thinking uses the YES/NO system. Lateral thinking does not

The very basis of vertical thinking is that you are not allowed to be wrong at any stage. That is the most important characteristic that defines the system. Each step must be fully justified and rest soundly on the preceding step. Vertical thinking is a selective type of thinking and it uses judgment. This judgment is based on the YES/NO system, and selection is by exclusion of all those ideas to which the NO label can be attached. Without the YES/NO system vertical thinking could not work. Vertical thinking is looking for what is right.

Lateral thinking works outside the YES/NO system. Lateral thinking is not looking for what is right but for what is different. Lateral thinking uses information in a way that is quite different from vertical thinking (as will be discussed later in this section) and the question of right or wrong does not arise. In the course of lateral thinking, you may have to use an idea which everyone knows to be wrong and which you yourself know to be wrong. Nor do you hold it in the belief that it may eventually prove to be right. Right and wrong simply do not apply.

With lateral thinking the only "wrong" is the arrogance or rigidity with which an idea is held. The nature of the idea itself does not matter at all.

Vertical thinking uses information for its meaning. Lateral thinking uses information for its effect in setting off new ideas

Vertical thinking is analytical. Lateral thinking is provocative. Vertical thinking is interested in where an idea comes from: this is the backward use of information. Lateral thinking is interested in where an idea leads to: this is the forward use of information. A vertical thinker will try to find out why an idea will not work so that he can reject it. A lateral thinker will try to see what can be made of the idea even if he knows it to be inadequate in its present form. Instead of looking to see why an idea is wrong, a lateral thinker looks to see what can be got out of it. Lateral thinking uses ideas in a catalytic fashion in order to trigger off new ideas and to bring about repatterning.

Vertical thinking is used *to describe* what has happened in one's own thinking. Lateral thinking is used *to make* something happen.

In vertical thinking one thing must follow directly from another. In lateral thinking one can make deliberate jumps

Vertical thinking seeks to establish continuity. Lateral thinking seeks to introduce discontinuity. In vertical thinking, one step follows directly from the preceding step in a logical sequence. In lateral thinking, one can make a completely unjustified jump. One does not have to make such a jump but one is allowed to. In vertical thinking there is a reason for saying something before it is said. In lateral thinking there may not be a reason for saying something until after it has been said. The point about the jumps in lateral thinking is that they are unjustified until *after* they have been made. In terms of the old pattern of ideas, the jump makes no sense but, once made, the jump can open up a new pattern which quickly justifies the jump.

In vertical thinking, one is uncomfortable if there is a gap. In lateral thinking, one may try hard to create such a gap in order to escape from the old ideas.

In vertical thinking, the conclusion must come after the evidence. In lateral thinking, the conclusion may come before the evidence. This is not to say that one adopts a conclusion and then seeks to justify it by rationalization. Such a procedure would imply an arrogant certainty in the conclusion that is the opposite of lateral thinking. The process is rather one of making a provocative jump to a new position and, once there, one is suddenly able to see things in a new way. The new way must of course prove itself by being effective.

Vertical thinking concentrates on what is relevant. Lateral thinking welcomes chance intrusions

Vertical thinking chooses what is to be considered. Anything else is rejected. This choice of what is relevant depends entirely on the original way of looking at the situation. Lateral thinking welcomes chance intrusions because it is difficult to change an idea from within itself. Lateral thinking encourages happy accidents because they can set off new patterns of ideas. Chance is one way of introducing that element of discontinuity that lateral thinking uses in order to bring about new ideas. In lateral thinking, nothing can be irrelevant. Even if something seems irrelevant in itself, it can still set off ideas when considered alongside the problem in hand.

Vertical thinking moves in the most likely directions. Lateral thinking explores the least likely

Vertical thinking proceeds along well-established patterns

because it is seeking proof and proof is most easily found by using such patterns. Vertical thinking is not used to seek out new ideas, and there is no reason for avoiding the obvious. Lateral thinking, on the other hand, seeks to avoid the obvious. This is not because novelty has any value in itself, but because the very obviousness of an idea may obscure a better idea which lies just beneath. By making a habit of exploring beyond the obvious, lateral thinking can come up with such ideas. If no new ideas emerge, then you can always go back to the obvious idea. There is nothing to be lost by exploring beyond it. In the final stage, there is no point in choosing an odd idea just for the sake of its oddity, but in the exploratory stage such odd ideas can be more worthwhile to follow than the obvious ones.

Vertical thinking is a closed procedure. Lateral thinking is open-ended

Vertical thinking promises at least a minimal result. Lateral thinking increases the chances of a maximal result but makes no promises. You can work through vertical thinking procedures and you will come up with some sort of answer, for this answer is only a way of relating the concepts with which you started out. With lateral thinking, you may come up with a brilliant answer or you may come up with nothing at all. You can never guarantee that lateral thinking will produce an answer which is good enough or new enough. It is always an open-ended probabilistic system. With a skilled lateral thinker, the chances that some sort of solution will emerge are high; but there can never be certainty.

This does not mean that one cannot use a probabilistic system for practical problem solving. One can and should do so. If no new solutions turn up, then one can always go back to whatever solutions are turned up by vertical thinking. One is no worse off than if one had never used lateral thinking. But if a brilliant solution does turn up, then one may be considerably better off. Creativity is always open-ended but one can very much *increase the chances of success* by developing skill in lateral thinking. It is like having three black balls and one white one in a bag. The chances of drawing out the white ball are small at first. If you go on dropping additional white balls into the bag then the chances get better and better. But no matter how many white balls there are in the bag at the end, you can never be absolutely sure of picking out a white ball. Dropping white balls into the bag is equivalent to acquiring skill in lateral thinking.

The use of lateral and vertical thinking

Since lateral thinking is an open-ended procedure, it might be supposed that a lot of time could be wasted while one waited for a brilliant solution to come about. It might be argued that it was more sensible to get one with vertical thinking even if the results were less spectacular. Such an attitude shows a misunderstanding of the nature of lateral thinking. Lateral thinking is not something that is to be used all the time. Lateral thinking introduces discontinuity or a change in direction. You cannot get anywhere by changing direction at each pace. But by changing direction at one point and then striding on in the new direction you can "go places." The striding is equivalent to vertical thinking, and the change of direction to lateral thinking. To refuse to use lateral thinking is to condemn oneself to moving always in the same direction, or at least until so many other people have changed direction that obviously you must follow them.

In practice, one might use lateral thinking some 5 percent of the time and vertical thinking 95 percent of the time. Even this figure is high for lateral thinking. It depends a good deal on the nature of the situation. If you have to come up with a new product, or you cannot solve a problem with vertical thinking, then you might spend a lot of time thinking laterally. But in the normal course of events, one might spend no more than three minutes a day thinking laterally about some problem. That is an amount of time anyone can afford, especially when the payoff can be huge. The actual time spent thinking laterally is much less important than the availability of the tool. Because this thinking tool is available (if one has learned how to use it), then one can face situations in a different way. One is less inclined to be rigid, or arrogant, or dogmatic. One is inclined to listen to other people's ideas and even explore them for what they are worth. It is rather like having a jack in the back of the car. You may never need to use it, but merely having it there gives you more confidence and flexibility in your travels.

In practice, one uses lateral and vertical thinking in alternation. Lateral thinking turns up an idea, vertical thinking develops it. Vertical thinking comes to a dead end, lateral thinking changes the approach so that vertical thinking can proceed again. Rarely does lateral thinking actually provide a solution by itself. Usually, it simply provides an approach or rescues someone who has been blocked by a particular idea.

When lateral thinking casts doubt on a well-established idea or concept, the intention is not to make that idea unusable. One has to use what ideas one has, otherwise it is impossible to proceed at all. What lateral thinking does is to open up the possibility of restructuring the idea in order to bring it up to date. It is not so much a matter of creating chronic dissatisfaction with current ideas, but of creating the hope of restructuring them.

Once one has acquired the habit of lateral thinking, the actual use of it is not confined to formal occasions or techniques but mingles naturally with the use of vertical thinking. But before that stage can be reached, one does have to pay some attention to the principles of lateral thinking and also develop some skill through practice. Otherwise one must rest content with whatever natural skill one might have in this matter.

Lateral thinking is of course concerned with thinking, with the generating of new ideas and new approaches, and with the escape from old ones. It is not a method for decision or for action. Once the ideas have been generated, one has to satisfy oneself as to their *usefulness* before putting them into action. To do this one can use the full rigor of vertical thinking. But you do need to have the ideas first before you can examine them.

The behavior of a patterning system

It is certainly possible to be creative or to use lateral thinking without having any knowledge of the basic information processes of the mind. One can use the creativity that comes along on a chance basis, one can encourage those habits of mind that seem to bring about creativity, or one can simply learn some creative technique.

But the need for creativity and the processes of creativity both arise from the nature of the mind as an information handling system. If one has an idea of the *broad characteristics* of the type of information system involved, then creativity changes from mysterious magic to predictable process. If one appreciates the limitations of the information system of mind, one comes to realize that the principles of lateral thinking are not empirical gimmicks but are logically necessary procedures. It is only by looking at the information system of mind that one can see *why it is logical to be illogical.*

The mind is a self-organizing information system. Self-organizing information systems are inevitably patterning systems. This is a broad class of information system, but it does have certain very definite characteristics. These characteristics determine the way the mind handles information, and hence the way we think.

Patterning systems are highly effective and they have certain immense advantages. These advantages arise directly from the nature of the system. But this same nature also gives rise to certain disadvantages or limitations. It is not possible to alter the system so as to retain the advantages but get rid of the disadvantages, because they are merely different ways of looking at the same process. A knife is useful because it is sharp. But because it is sharp it is also dangerous. It is not possible to retain the usefulness and get rid of the danger. The best one can do is to learn the nature of the knife, and then to use it so as to enjoy the sharpness while minimizing the danger. Logical or vertical thinking enables us to make use of the mind system, and lateral thinking helps to minimize the dangers of the system.

What is a self-organizing system?

An externally organized system takes things and arranges them in a certain order. An externally organized information system takes information and puts it together in a certain way. A computer is an externally organized system. Rules of behavior are fed into the computer in the form of a program, and this program decides how the computer is going to handle the information that is fed into it.

In a self-organizing system the information arranges itself into some order. The mind does not organize information but provides an *environment for incoming information to organize itself into patterns*.

Models

It is not possible in this book to go into a full explanation of the mechanism of mind. Those who require fuller details might care to read *The Mechanism of Mind* (Simon & Schuster, New York, 1969) (Jonathan Cape, London, 1969). It is helpful, however, to consider two simple models here.

Take a white towel and lay it out smoothly on a flat surface. From a bowl of blue ink, take a spoonful at a time and pour it on to the towel at any place. The towel represents a recording or memory surface. The ink represents an *input* to that surface. The ink stain represents the *record of memory* of that input. Since every point of the towel surface is unique, the place where the ink is poured represents a unique set of points. Thus, each different place stained by the ink represents a new and unique piece of input that is a unique piece of information. After a time, the towel will be covered with an array of blue spots which will represent the complete record of all the information that has come onto that surface. The crucial point is that the record will be *exact*. The absorbent nature of the towel will ensure that the ink *stays exactly where it is put*. Thus, the ink stain will cover the same unique set of points that were originally covered by the ink, and the surface will be a simple passive record of all the information that has come in. Each piece of information is recorded separately in its original state. Furthermore, the time at which the information arrived (that is, the spoonful of ink was poured onto a certain spot) will make no difference. If there are two ink stains a few inches apart, it makes no difference which one arrived first. Nor is there any way of telling which one arrived first.

Thus, the towel represents an accurate information recording surface. It is accurate because it does *not* actually do anything to the information except record it. If you wanted to do something to the information you would have to do it yourself. The towel acts like the memory of a computer which faithfully records input information. Then there is the computer processor which takes this information and uses it. In fact, the processor can use it only if the information has been recorded faithfully (that is, if the ink-stain has stayed where it was put).

Consider now a rather different type of surface. In place of the towel, put a large flat dish of gelatin. This time, heat the bowl of ink. Otherwise the procedure is exactly as before. A spoonful at a time is taken from the bowl and poured onto the surface of the gelatin. The spot where it is poured and the sequence of spots can be exactly the same as for the towel. What happens now is that while the ink is hot it dissolves away some of the gelatin. After a few moments, the cooled ink and the melted gelatin are poured off the dish. What is left is a shallow depression in the surface of the gelatin. This is the record or memory of where the ink was placed.

If the ink is placed each time in a completely different spot on this gelatin surface, after a time the surface of the gelatin will be covered with a number of small depressions. The general effect would be similar to the towel model. But if ink is poured onto the surface just next to an already existing depression, then the hot ink will flow into that depression, making it even deeper. After a while, this erosion will result in channels, just as a landscape is eroded by rainfall into streams and rivers. The significant point is that the ink no longer stays where it is placed but flows away along a channel to a new place. This means that the information is no longer recorded faithfully (that is, kept in the same place) but is actually *changed by the surface*. Furthermore, as the ink flows along a channel it deepens that channel even more, thus making it increasingly likely to divert further incoming information.

Unlike the towel surface, which was a passive and accurate recording surface, the gelatin surface does things to the incoming information. The surface does not actually organize the information, but it provides an opportunity or environment for the information to organize itself into patterns. These patterns are the channels in the surface. Information (ink) arriving at one part of the channel flows along to the end of the channel.

The gelatin surface is an information-processing system because you usually get *more* than you put in. This is because ink placed at one spot actually gets to flow through several other spots as well. Compared with the towel surface the gelatin surface is actually a very bad recording surface, because it does not preserve things as they are but alters them. The paradox is that it is a good information processor precisely because it is a bad memory.

The gelatin surface provides an opportunity for information to organize itself into patterns. Thus it is a self-organizing system. But what is actually responsible for this organizing? The surprisingly simple answer is *time*. The sequence in which the different spots on the gelatin surface receive the spoonfuls of ink will totally determine the way the channels form. With the towel surface the sequence in which the ink was placed at the different spots did not matter at all; but with the gelatin surface this sequence is all important since it is the basis of the patterns that arise.

The gelatin surface is but a simple model of a self-organizing information system, yet the implications of its behavior are huge.

1. The system provides an opportunity for information to organize itself into patterns.
2. Information is processed by proceeding along the existing patterns (channels).
3. The sequence in which information arrives determines the patterns that form.

What is a pattern?

"Where any state is preferentially followed by another state, that is a pattern."

Consider the points in Figure 2–1. If there is a free choice in proceeding from point A to any other point, then there is no pattern. But if there is a preference for proceeding from point A to point B, then there is a pattern. The pattern can of course carry on if at point B there is a preference for proceeding to point C and so on.

A road is a pattern. Theoretically, an automobile could proceed in any direction. But its actual preference of direction is determined by the availability of the road. As the car moves along the road, it changes its position with regard to some reference system. This change of state is taking place in a preferred direction.

In the gelatin model, ink placed at one spot tends to flow along a channel eroded in the gelatin surface. As it flows along, the ink, like the automobile on a road, is changing its position on the surface. Since a change in position on the gelatin surface is equivalent to a change in the information input, so the flowing ink gives rise to one information state after another in the preferential manner determined by the channel. This is then a pattern of information or, in human terms, a train of ideas or thoughts.

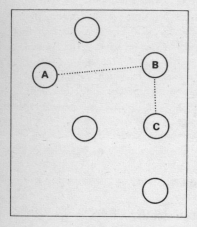

Figure 2–1.

Though the road itself is a pattern on the landscape, there may also be a further pattern in the way a road is used. If you are driving to a familiar destination and you come to a junction in the road, you will take the branch with which you are familiar. The different segments of your route will hang together to give a complete pattern. A pattern is where separate things hang together or follow one another.

The usual use of the word *pattern* is unfortunately rather limited. A pattern on wallpaper or dress fabric is the repetition of some design. One says there is a pattern when, having seen one part of the design, one expects this part to be repeated and one turns out to be correct in this expectation. The confusing point is that repetition itself has nothing to do with a pattern; but expectancy, or familiarity, does. It is not the fact that you have the same design over and over again that makes the pattern, but the fact that *you know what to expect*. A tune is a pattern because you know what to expect, not because it repeats the same note over and over again.

In an established pattern, if you stop at any point there is always ahead of you *a preferred point*. Thus, if a pattern is interrupted at any point, there is always an expectancy of its completion. Figure 2–2 shows an outline figure obscured by an inkblot. The exposed part of the figure leads one to expect the completion of a circle. Even proceeding from the visual figure to the name *circle* is itself a pattern.

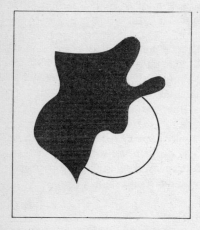

Figure 2–2.

The light in my bathroom is switched on by pulling on a cord which hangs from a ceiling switch just inside the door. There is quite a high step at the entrance. The usual pattern is to climb the step and pull the cord to switch on the light. This is so well established a pattern that when someone else has left the light on I still climb the step and pull the cord, thus actually turning the light *off*.

The numbers 352–55 are part of a telephone number, and one expects the missing numbers to give the whole pattern 352–5572. But the number itself is part of another pattern which includes the expectancy of speaking to a certain person. And that person himself with all his characteristics is another pattern. *A pattern is anything where items of information hang together and so give an expectancy.*

The mind functions because it is a *pattern-creating* and *pattern-using system.*

All the characteristics of a pattern arise from the basic definition that *a given state passes preferentially to another state.* It is because of this that patterns are:

1. Recognizable.
2. Repeatable.
3. Give rise to expectancy.
These are but different aspects of the same thing.

Advantages of a patterning system

A pattern provides a channel for change, for moving from
one state to another in an above-chance manner. The
advantages of a patterning system are huge. It is only possible
to outline some of them here.

1. Selection. At any moment the human mind is surrounded
by a mass of data. It could potentially react to each bit of
data in the environment, although it would be completely
overwhelmed by the vast amount of data available. But
having started at one point (that particular point depending
on what had been happening just before), the mind is guided
by a pattern to respond to only *some* of the available data.
The mind appears *to pick out a significant pattern.* All it is
really doing is following such an already established pattern,
which allows it to pick out the relevant data. Figure 2–3

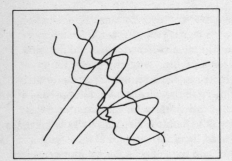

Figure 2–3.

shows an array of lines. Some of the lines actually form the
outline of a face. It is a very simple matter to pick out this
face, because one follows an established pattern. Similarly,
an experienced accountant looking at a balance sheet can
quickly pick out a pattern from what would simply be confusing data to someone else.

2. Triggers. In order to break a large plate-glass window, you
would have to hurl a big stone at it with considerable force.
But if you were to use a gun, then the force needed would

only be that little pressure required to pull the trigger. That is because with a gun you are simply setting off a preset chain of events which follow one another once they have been set off. *A pattern is a preset chain of events.* A pattern allows one to get beyond the usual limits of cause and effect. With a pattern, the same "cause" may have totally different effects depending on *the patterns which are triggered off.* Two apparently similar people are listening to the news on the radio. There is a news item about a flare-up of hostilities in the Middle East. One man picks up the phone to cancel a planned holiday. The other man picks up the phone to buy stock in an oil company with Alaskan wells. The cause has been the same in both cases. But the "effect" is quite different and depends on the preset patterns that have been triggered off. In a physical system, the nature of the cause is very important because it allows one to predict the effect. In a patterning system, however, the nature of the cause is not nearly so important as the nature of the patterns which might be triggered off. In a patterning system, one can go far beyond what might be effected by a simple cause. Cause and effect no longer have much meaning; one looks instead for points of change which can trigger off patterns.

3. Code communication. If you had to transfer information piece by piece, it would take a very long time. An engineer ordering a particular machine tool would have to describe its shape, size, and function in at least enough detail to distinguish it from all other available machines. But with a code communication system, all he needs to do is to look at the catalog number of the machine he wants and use this number to order one. The catalog number acts as a trigger to set off in the receiver all the information that the engineer would otherwise have had to supply. A code-communication system allows one to transfer huge amounts of information very fast and with little effort. But a code-communication system depends on preset arrangements of information (patterns) which can be triggered off by the code word. Ordinary language is of course the best example of a code-communication system. But, even when communicating not with people but with the environment, one has preset patterns which can be triggered off by certain clues which act to set off patterns. Words or clues are no more than the beginning of complete patterns which the mind then completes by itself.

4. *Anticipation.* A pattern allows one to react to an event before the event has occurred. If you see a car blocking the road, you do not have to wait until you hit the car before deciding that you ought to brake. By extending the pattern, you can get ahead of the actual event and react accordingly. If you see signs of inflation in the economy you could, if you were in the government, suggest steps to control it before it became severe. Similarly, if you saw anti-inflationary measures being taken you could, as a business executive, react to this pattern before it harmed your business. A patterning system pulls things out of their real time sequence, and so allows one to react not only to things but also to the anticipation of them.

5. *Maps.* Basically, a patterning system allows one to carry around a personal map of the environment. This map may be fragmented into separate pieces but, like a map torn into small pieces, you can still make use of the piece relevant to the area in which you find yourself.

6. *Labels and values.* A label or a name is the code word for a particular pattern. One normally uses the code word to call forth the whole pattern. But you can short-circuit or bypass the whole pattern by attaching a value label (good, bad, unreliable, and so on) to the code word. Thus if a particular employee had proved unreliable in the past, you would not have to bring to mind the full details of his unreliability but would simply attach the label unreliable to his name, and so create a new short-circuit pattern.

Disadvantages of a patterning system

The basic advantages of a patterning system are pretty obvious, even though the full implication of these advantages is not so obvious. The disadvantages of a patterning system are rather less obvious. The full implications of these disadvantages are quite difficult to appreciate. This is because we live inside a patterning system and cannot look at it objectively.

1. *Lack of choice.* It is easy to accept the notion that a patterning system provides an internal map which we can use to find our way around the environment. But we suppose that the map is only an aid and that we are really free to go

here or there. Figure 2–4 is a diagram with a number of
lettered points which represent states of information or
ideas. An established pattern links A–B–C–D. A less well
established pattern links A–G–H–F. We suppose that if we
were at point A we would recognize the dominant pattern
and also the less dominant one, and yet we would be free to
choose to go to M instead of B or G. Unfortunately that is
not how patterning systems work. A patterning system could
never work if the preference for passing from one state to
another was *simply optional.* In fact, one would proceed
straight along the dominant pattern path and not even be
aware of the other possibilities. Indecision can occur when
there are two competing patterns both so well established
that fluctuations in mood, et cetera, can throw now one and
now the other into dominance. But where there is established
dominance, there is no question of alternatives.

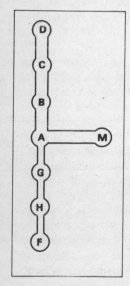

Figure 2–4.

2. *Fine choice.* In a horse race it is not difficult to shift one's
choice from the favorite to the second favorite and so on
down the line. In a patterning system, however, the best
established pattern has a complete dominance no matter
how close in establishment an alternative pattern may be. As
information proceeds along one pattern pathway, the other
pattern is as completely ignored as if it did not exist. Thus, a
person looking at a situation in one way may be completely

unable to see an alternative point of view until it is presented to him. Once he has seen it, he can then acknowledge that it is very nearly as likely as his own point of view.

3. Blocked by openness. In a patterning system, the biggest danger is being blocked by the simple fact that there is nothing in the way. One has no choice but to follow a well-established pattern along to its end. It is not possible to branch off at some point and follow an alternative pattern. This process is shown in Figure 2–5. It is extremely difficult to break away from a satisfactory view of things to find a better one. It is very much easier if there is a problem situation and one is actually looking around for some pattern to follow. Lack of suitable patterns can prevent an appropriate response

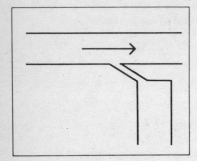

Figure 2–5.

in a patterning system, but *availability of unsuitable patterns* is a much *greater danger.* After all, one can acquire new patterns but it is extremely difficult to disrupt an established pattern. The dilemma is that a person poorly equipped with a repertoire of patterns will be unable to look at data in a *meaningful* way. On the other hand, a person well equipped with patterns will be unable to look at the data in a *new* way.

4. Cutting across patterns. It is easier to establish a completely new pattern than to cut across an old pattern, using part of it but exchanging the rest for something new. This is often seen in an argument or bargaining situation where it proves impossible to change a particular concept, but where agreement can be reached if a new concept is introduced. It is puite easy to combine two patterns to form a larger pattern, but not so easy to combine bits of established patterns. To do this, one has first to break up the established patterns into smaller pieces and then to combine the pieces. An amusing example of this is the ancient mythological figure of the centaur. Here the legless body of a man is combined with the headless body of a horse. The resultant creature has two thoraxes and two abdomens. If one does have to change a pattern (a concept, idea, and the like) it is much easier to change from outside than from within it. It is very difficult to start off along the pattern A–B–C shown in Figure 2–6 and hope to branch off at B to create the new pattern A–B–F. It would be much easier to create the pattern F–E separately and then to show that it could link up at B.

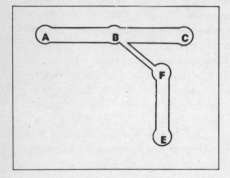

Figure 2–6.

5. Snap-over. It is easier to snap over to a new pattern than to try to modify an old one. On the other hand, it is not possible to establish a sort of midpoint average between an old pattern and a new one. Either the old pattern holds up, or there is a snap-over to a new one, or there may be an alternative between the two. This snap-over process is seen in insight where the old way of looking at things suddenly gives place to a new way. The paradox is that *a big change is much easier than a small change in a patterning system.*

6. Polarization. This follows from the snap-over effect. It is easier to have two distinct patterns than modifications of the same pattern. Thus two distinct ways of looking at a situation evolve and grow stronger, whereas partially similar ways coalesce into the same way.

7. Patterns get larger. Patterns tend to get larger and larger. Small patterns link up to give longer sequences. The process is always toward getting longer, never toward getting shorter. When a short pattern is triggered by incoming information, one has to go back to this information in order to continue with a new pattern. When a very long pattern gets triggered, one continues with this pattern and has no need for further information. The longer the pattern, the more likely it is to diverge from reality. Old people tend to have very rigid views, and this is because the pattern chains have become so long that they no longer reflect immediate experience. Thus the views of an old trade unionist may be quite out of keeping with the fluctuations of a changing industrial situation. The same is just as true of a marketing manager.

8. Patterns grow by extension. The natural tendency is for a pattern to grow by extension. Bits are added on. Or the pattern may come to link up with another pattern. It is like finding one's way around by road in a new town. All the time, you extend the familiar segments of road that you know. It may be years before you discover that you have been taking a very roundabout route between two places which are linked much more directly. When one faces a situation, one is already committed to some pattern in the way one looks at the situation. So anything new one learns is tacked on to extend this original pattern. It is extremely difficult to put aside this starting pattern and develop a new one.

9. Assumptions. In order to be able to see a situation at all, one has to see it in terms of some basic starting pattern. This seems so fundamental that one does not realize that it is actually an arbitrary arrangement of information, for it seems to be the very situation itself. Thus, it would be very difficult to look at strikes as a spur to industrial productivity by squeezing profits between high labor costs and market-pegged sales prices. By definition, strikes are an interruption in the industrial process and hence in productivity.

10. Patterns drain off meaning. A well-established pattern *reduces* a situation to that pattern. Theoretically, it may be possible to look at the situation in a great number of different ways but, in practice, it is not the richness of the situation that matters but the presence or absence of well-established patterns.

11. Mistakes. Patterning systems are very open to mistakes. If two completely different situations start out in the same way, then it is very easy to use the wrong pattern. Some

26

patterns do have code names, words, or labels, but in order to apply these one has first to identify the pattern. This one does, whether or not there is a code word, from the *initial stages* of the pattern. In a patterning system, there can be no protection at all against mistaken identity of patterns. If there were a hundred items in a sequence in a pattern, you could wait until you had seen ninety-nine before identifying the pattern, but even then you could be wrong about the last item. In actual practice, one tries to identify a pattern much earlier and is even more likely to be wrong. It is not a question of making a mistake but of two situations starting out in the same way.

12. Inappropriate patterns. A patterning system is a probabilities system. By identifying the first part of a pattern, one bets that the rest will be as expected. If one cannot easily identify a pattern, then, rather than be left in a patternless void, one searches around for a clue that will set off some pattern or other. This "nearest" pattern may be highly inappropriate, and by using it one may be far worse off than if one had not been able to identify a pattern at all.

13. Difficulty in prediction. The same external situation may trigger completely different patterns in different people depending on their individual experience. Because of this, it is not possible to predict a reaction by study of the stimulus. In a nonpattern system the reaction could be determined by a study of the stimulus, but in a patterning system this is not so because the stimulus merely acts as a trigger.

14. Importance of sequence of arrival of information. The fundamental characteristic of a patterning system is that the sequence of arrival of information determines the patterns in which it is arranged. The significance of this point is discussed later on in this chapter.

15. Continuity. Another fundamental characteristic of a patterning system is continuity. At any point in a pattern, the tendency is to continue along that pattern. There is no mechanism for breaking off. Once a pattern emerges, the tendency is for that pattern to continue and to become even more firmly established. In a way, a patterning system is a continuity system. A patterning system enables one to take some information input and *to go further with it*. A patterning system functions on the assumption that things in the future will continue to be as they have been in the past. This continuity aspect will also be discussed again later in the chapter.

Other features of a patterning system

These other features are neither advantages nor dis-advantages, but they arise from the nature of a patterning system.

1. Importance of escaping from dominant pattern. Since the dominant pattern suppresses all other patterns, if one can escape from this dominant pattern one is quite likely to find an alternative pattern or way of looking at a situation. This is an important point, because one of the objects of lateral thinking is to generate new ideas simply by escaping from old ones. It is not a matter of escaping from the old idea and then generating a whole number of new ideas only one of which may be useful. Because of the nature of a patterning system, mere escape from an old idea can often reveal a new idea which was really *there all the time* but was not available.

2. Importance of change of entry point. The entry point is the point at which one starts along some pattern. Figure 2–7 shows a diagram representing a simple pattern. In each segment,

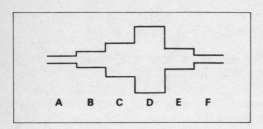

Figure 2–7.

the width of the road indicates the preference in favor of moving on to that segment. The overall preference is also to move forward rather than backward along a segment already traversed. If one enters at D then one moves to C and then to B and then to A. If, however, one had entered at C in the first place then one would have moved to D and then to E and F. Thus by a simple change of entry point, one can end up at a totally different place. This is an important point

28

because, though one can do little about changing patterns, there are ways in which one can alter the entry point. Figure 2–8 shows how this sort of thing could happen in a marketing situation. If the entry point is at "sales falling," then the

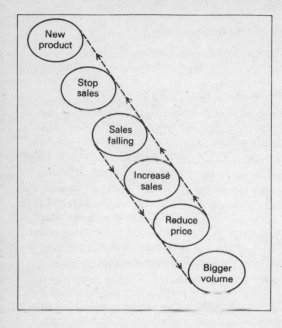

Figure 2–0.

sequence might go: remedy this by increasing sales. How? By lowering prices and so increasing volume sales. If, however, one entered at the "reduced prices," point, the sequence might go as follows: increase sales; but sales are falling so one might have to go on lowering prices. Perhaps it might be better to stop sales of this item and to develop a new product.

3. Importance of starting at end rather than beginning. Jumping to the end instead of working along from the beginning may be a particular case of the change of entry point. Figure 2–9 shows a rectangular figure of paper. How could you cut this piece of paper so that the rectangle might become one-third as long again as the original figure but with the same area? The usual approach is to see how one could make the rectangle longer by some cut as shown. This is quite difficult to do. A different approach is shown in Figure 2–10. Here the approach is to jump to the end and say: "If the rectangle

Figure 2-9.

is one-third longer but of the same area, then it must be one-third thinner, so let us start by making it thinner." To do this one cuts off a slice. Then one simply divides the slice and adds it to the end.

Starting at the end instead of the beginning may be more than just changing the entry point into the same pattern. When you begin to solve a problem, there is no guarantee that the pattern you start with will ever lead to the solution point. On the other hand, if you start with the solution point and then work backward, there is a guarantee that your pattern will end at the solution point. There is, however, no guarantee that it will join up with your starting situation. On the whole, a starting situation is much more open to choice than a solution situation, so it can be better to start at the end. This would be true even in a non-patterning system, but it is par-

Figure 2-10.

ticularly true in a patterning system since, once started, a pattern tends to carry one along even past the side turning that would have led to the solution. (See Figure 2–11.)

A rather obvious example of starting from the end rather than the beginning is the case of a person wishing to raise capital in a time of inflation. Instead of considering how he can raise the money, he considers whether he can pay it back at the end. Since, in an inflationary period, a loan will be worth less when paid back than when borrowed, he might prefer to raise capital in this way.

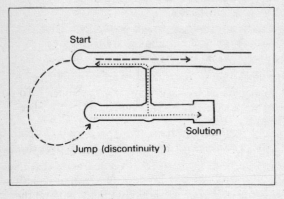

Figure 2–11.

4. Importance of provocation. Provocation implies discontinuity. Instead of following along a pattern or moving smoothly from one pattern to another, one makes an unjustified jump to a new point. Various techniques for achieving this sort of discontinuity are described later. This provocative jump is somewhat similar to jumping to a new entry point or to the end point, except that it is more extreme. The new point may have nothing at all to do with the pattern being used or indeed with the situation. Once the new point has been reached, one works backward from it to link it up with the situation under consideration. The linkup will allow a new approach to the problem. Instead of having to approach the problem through the old pattern, one jumps to a new and disconnected point and then works back toward the problem. Provocation and discontinuity of this sort work in a patterning system because the usual pattern is neither the only possible one nor the best one. The provocative jump is unjustified before it is made, but once it has been made it can reveal a new approach which fully justifies it. Figure

2–11 shows the usual way a problem might be developed and then what happens when a discontinuous jump is made. Provocation is necessary because continuity is so strong in a patterning system that any change can only be brought about by deliberate or chance induced discontinuity.

Time of arrival of information patterns. Restructuring

A business organization grows over a period of time. Things happen to it and change it. New opportunities arise, new ideas, new personalities. The market changes. All these things can be regarded as new inputs to the organization. They can be regarded as new information.

Over the course of his life, a person gradually acquires additional information. He may acquire it firsthand by experience or secondhand from the experience of others. The important thing is that things happen one after another in a sequence.

The way information arrives piece by piece is character- istic of science, of civilizations, of cultures. In fact, it is characteristic of anything which exists over a period of time and which is open to receiving information (input) over that period.

Although information arrives piece by piece over a period of time, one has to make the best use of it at any given moment. One has no idea whether there is going to be any further information on any particular matter or when it might arrive. So one makes the best use of information already available. The available information becomes organ- ized into patterns which are then found to be useful and so survive, or useless and gradually atrophy. The criterion of usefulness depends on the particular field under considera- tion.

A simple model using the sequential arrival of plastic pieces can show what happens in this type of system. The pieces arrive *one after the other*. Yet at each stage the person to whom they are given is required to arrange them in the best possible order (that is, make the best sense of them). The best possible order is here·defined as a shape which can be simply and accurately described to someone who cannot actually see what is being done. This definition of "best" is equivalent to a *usable* arrangement.

The two pieces shown in Figure 2–12a are presented first. They are usually arranged as a rectangle (Figure 2–12b).

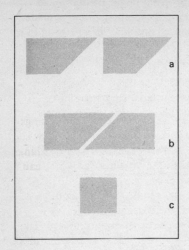

Figure 2–12a, b, c.

Another piece is now provided (Figure 2–12c). After some hesitation, this piece is added on to the previous arrangement to give a longer rectangle as shown in Figure 2–13a.

Finally two more pieces are added (Figure 2–13b). There is now great difficulty in arranging the pieces to give a simple shape. Attempts usually end up with one of the two arrangements shown in Figure 2–14, both of which are inadequate.

In order to proceed, one has to go back to the second stage, which was perfectly correct, and restructure it to give a square. The third stage is then absurdly easy since the square is simply enlarged. This sequence is shown in Figure 2–15.

This may seem a simple game with plastic pieces, but if one abstracts the processes involved one can see that they apply

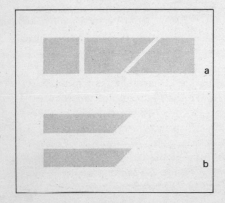

Figure 2–13a, b.

Figure 2–14.

Figure 2–15.

34

to any system in which information arrives piece by piece and yet in which one is required to make the best use of what is already available at each stage. The following points can be made:

1. The arrangement tends to grow by continuity. If one can add the new piece to the existing arrangement one does so. This is seen in the adding of the small square to the original rectangle to give the longer rectangle.

2. The first rectangle is undoubtedly the best arrangement of available pieces. The second rectangle is also the best arrangement of available pieces (given the existence of the first one). Thus, one has been absolutely correct at both stages. And yet one cannot proceed further. So being right at each stage is not enough.

3. In order to be able to proceed, one has to restructure an arrangement of information which was the best at the time it was made. There is no question of having to re-structure a wrong or inadequate arrangement. It is a matter of having to restructure an arrangement which was (at the time it was made) the best possible one. Though this is a simple point, it is very important. It is easy enough to accept that an inadequate arrangement should be improved; it is much more difficult to accept that something which was very good should be restructured and changed.

4. In the second stage, when the longer rectangle was made, there was no incentive at all to see if an alternative structure such as the square was also possible. It is only *subsequent* events which make the square a preferable alternative. The rectangle is more fitted to the *past* information and the square to the *future* information, but one cannot at the time have any idea of what the future information is going to be. In fact, there was no reason to look for an alternative arrangement or to prefer that arrangement if it had been found.

5. With hindsight it becomes obvious that at the second stage it would have been worthwhile to look for all possible alternative arrangements even if one returned to the rectangle.

6. At the third stage one might have reached the solution by playing around with all the pieces, but it was clearly easier to discard the new pieces and see how one could restructure a previous arrangement that was being taken for granted.

7. A few people reach the solution by taking the two final pieces and arranging them as shown in Figure 2–16. They then see whether the old pieces can be fitted into this new frame. This is an interesting diversion. It means that if the new information is sufficient one can try arranging it *on its own* and then fitting in the old arrangements rather than working the other way round.
8. If the five pieces are all presented at once there is much more chance of reaching the solution, because there is no commitment to build on an existing arrangement.

All these observations can be summed up by saying that in an information system where the information arrives in a time sequence, the arrangement at any moment can never make the best use of available information. This is because the time sequence itself has played a large part in the current

Figure 2–16.

arrangement. And the "best" arrangement should depend on the nature of the information alone. This principle applies directly to patterns which are but arrangements brought about by the time sequence of arrival of information.

The importance of the time sequence in which pieces of information arrive is shown in a particularly striking manner by another set of plastic pieces. As before, the pieces are presented in a certain time sequence, and the task is to arrange them at each stage to give a recognizable shape.

The process is shown in Figure 2–17. The first two pieces are arranged to give a rectangle. Then the next two pieces are presented. These are put together to give a rectangle similar to the first one, and the two rectangles are pushed together to give a large rectangle. But when the next piece arrives there is great trouble in doing anything with it.

The same plastic pieces can, however, be presented in a

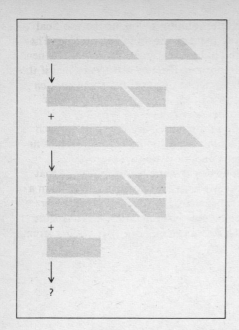

Figure 2-17.

different time sequence as in Figure 2-18. This time, the two long pieces are presented first and at once are arranged to give a rectangle. The two shorter pieces are presented next and they get added to the first rectangle to give a longer one. There is now no difficulty in fitting in the last piece, which is simply added to give a still longer rectangle.

The point is that this final arrangement *could* have been arrived at the first time, but the different sequence in which the pieces were presented makes this obvious arrangement very difficult. This may seem surprising, but it is what happens.

There is, in fact, another arrangement of the pieces in Figure 2-19, but this involves the same sort of restructuring as shown with the previous example.

The plastic pieces as such are not very important, but they do serve to characterize the behavior of a broad class of information systems. This includes any system in which information arrives over a period of time and yet has to be arranged to make the best sense at each stage. If this assembly is retained as a memory or as a pattern (that is, an expectation based on memory), then the free arrangement of the contained pieces is not possible. So, in this sort of system, the commitment to an arrangement that was the best

Figure 2–18.

at the time prevents the free use of contained information. The best use of the information would of course be the free use. This leads on to the simple statement of a law which applies to patterning systems such as the mind.

de Bono's first law:

"AN IDEA CAN NEVER BE THE BEST ARRANGEMENT OF AVAILABLE
INFORMATION"

The law is stated in absolute terms, for it is theoretically impossible to achieve the best arrangement of available

Figure 2–19.

38

information in an idea. The law is not meant to encourage hesitancy or indecision or a futile search for the absolute. On the contrary, one uses ideas in a practical manner. What the law implies is that one cannot regard any idea as absolute, and that there is always a need to try to restructure an idea in order to get a better one. The law is not intended to diminish the value of current ideas but to increase the incentive to restructure them.

One can make two points about a patterning system:
1. The arrangement of information is only one of several alternative arrangements so it is always *possible* to restructure.
2. Because the current arrangement of information can never make the best use of available information, it is *necessary* to try to restructure in order to bring the arrangement up to date.

Restructuring

Restructuring means putting together in a different way information that is already available. This restructuring process is characteristic of a patterning system such as the human mind. The process is usually a sudden one since there is a snap-over from one pattern arrangement to another. It is not a matter of gradual modification.

In the human mind, the restructuring switchover is apparent in the twin processes of humor and insight. In both cases, there is this sudden switchover from one way of looking at things to another.

Bob Hope: I had a very bad Christmas last year. I was given just four golf clubs . . . and only two of them had swimming pools.

Professor to law student: You are only engaged to your fiancée, yet you maintain it would be adultery if I seduced her?
Student: Yes, sir.
Professor: But you are not actually married.
Student: No, but *you* are.

Two people are attempting to guess the weight of a cake. The person who comes closer to the actual weight wins and takes the cake.
The first person says one pound.

The second person says two pounds.
The actual weight is one pound, four ounces, so the first person wins.

This seems very straightforward. But is it? If one makes a small insight switchover, a rather different result can be obtained. The second person obviously thinks the cake weighs more than the one pound estimated by the first person. But if he gives his actual estimation of two pounds then he splits the difference between one and two pounds with the first person. With an actual weight of anything more than a pound and a half, he wins; with anything less, he loses. But

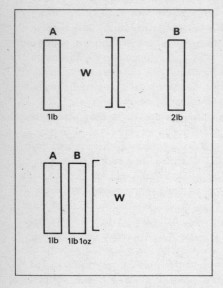

Figure 2–20.

if he thought the weight was likely to be more than a pound, he should really have said one pound, one ounce, in which case he would have won at *all* weights over a pound. In effect, by not realizing that he was actually trying to win the cake instead of making the best possible estimate, he threw away a great advantage (and in this case the cake). The process is shown in Figure 2–20. I have actually used this situation on many occasions with professional problem solvers (such as OR people), and hardly any of them made this *insight* switchover.

The restructuring phenomenon is not a luxury in a patterning system but an absolute necessity. Without insight, restructuring patterns could never be brought up to date with available information. If patterns grew only by extension they would get further and further from reality (as defined by all the information available). Without insight, restructuring a pattern could be adequate only when the information had been considerate enough to arrive in exactly the right sequence.

Insight restructuring is the mechanism for updating patterns to make them fit available information. Unfortunately, insight restructuring is extremely elusive and cannot be brought about at will. Nor have we developed any thinking tools to bring about this restructuring.

Lateral thinking is directed toward bringing about this insight restructuring. The need for lateral thinking arises from the nature of the patterning system of mind. The methods of lateral thinking are also based on the continuity of this system and the effects of introducing discontinuity.

In theory, insight restructuring could come about without any significant new input of information. It could simply be a putting together of old information in a new way. In practice, insight restructuring comes about only when some new information does not fit into the old pattern. When a lot of such information has accumulated, there is a chance that the pattern might be changed. This might seem an efficient process for updating patterns, and many people do actually feel that there is no need to try to generate new ideas because they will eventually come about of their own accord. The trouble with this *natural* updating is threefold.

1. The new information which should cause restructuring can often be distorted and fitted into the old pattern.
2. If the new information can be viewed only through the old pattern, only those parts of it which fit the old pattern will be accepted (a myth situation).
3. Unless the new information is abundant or powerful it will simply be ignored.

What this amounts to is that the natural restructuring of a pattern to bring it up to date always lags far behind the possible restructuring in terms of available information. It is this time lag which is so important. It may be months or years or even decades. In the business world where timing, quickness of reaction, and initiative are so vital a part of the process, one cannot simply wait for natural updating.

AN IDEA WILL CHANGE OF ITS OWN ACCORD LONG AFTER IT
COULD HAVE BEEN CHANGED

Summary

It is best to pause here before going on to the rest of the book. Having read and understood this chapter, one can forget about it. The chapter has been about patterning systems: about their advantages, disadvantages, and characteristics. The principles derived from these considerations apply directly to the way the mind handles information. There is nothing mysterious about them. They refer to the elementary behavior of any self-organizing information system.

As one looks at the behavior of the human mind, the patterning processes are sometimes perfectly obvious, but at other times they seem blurred by the illusion of direct choice.

It is suggested that the reader does not try to translate the processes and methods discussed in the rest of the book into patterning behavior. This could be very confusing. It is better to thoroughly acquaint oneself with the behavior in a patterning universe and not try to make a direct point-for-point translation.

The principles and methods of lateral thinking are indeed based upon the behavior of patterning systems, but there is no necessity to understand this behavior. The validity of lateral thinking depends on its empirical usefulness, not on its derivation. One can use lateral thinking because it makes sense and because it serves a purpose. There is no need to appreciate that the patterning nature of mind makes it essential.

By understanding the functional basis of lateral thinking all one acquires is a realization of the need for it, a greater confidence in its use, and the ability to do more than simply follow the specific methods. As with cooking, one can understand the chemistry of it, use the recipes, get someone else to cook, or eat in restaurants.

What can one do about thinking?   3

If one considers the brain as a special channel through which information flows (see Figure 3–1), then the information that comes in as data, evidence, appreciation of a situation, goes out as action, choice, decision, reaction, problem solving, and so on. The brain is a device for changing the nature of information and the process of change is called thinking. What can one do about thinking?

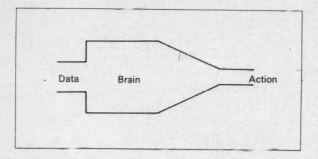

Data   Brain   Action

Figure 3–1.

1. Wait

You can sit around until information sorts itself out. You can sit around and wait until the pressure of information or circumstance is so strong that a course of action is decided for you. You can wait until some chance set of circumstances triggers off an idea. You can wait until someone tells you what to do. You can wait until your mood has changed to the extent that a course of action becomes clear.

2. Expose

Instead of waiting, you can expose yourself to circumstances by collecting information. You collect the information and then you allow yourself to react to it. Instead of waiting passively, you expose yourself to a small but highly significant part of the environment. This exposure may take the form of collecting facts and figures and reports, or it may consist in exposing yourself to the expert knowledge of others.

3. Borrow

You could borrow your ideas and your reaction patterns from others who appear to be in similar circumstances to you. This imitation does not involve understanding the reaction, evaluating it, or knowing the information on which it is based. One simply learns the reaction pattern as one might learn to use efficiently a machine one did not really understand.

4. Organize

You could organize the incoming information in ways which would make it easier for you to react to it. Just as an accountant organizes his information in such a way that it leads directly to reaction patterns, so you can categorize, classify, and identify in order to make it easier to trigger off standard reaction patterns.

5. Process

You can process information by using standard processing devices, such as mathematical techniques. Such techniques are no more than reliable change procedures. You translate your information into a suitable form and then allow it to run through the preset processing machine, and at the end you have changed your information into a form which is much easier to react to.

6. Clarify

You can try to find out how you are reacting to the information. This means trying to set out your thoughts in some sort of notation (reports, lists, diagrams, et cetera) and then reacting to this. You could also use another person to reflect back to you the way you are thinking. This sort of clarification allows you to react not only to the original information but to your reaction to it.

In all these cases, the basic process is the reaction to information. One needs to pay attention to the collection of information and then to the various tools for processing it, in order to reach a point where an appropriate reaction is triggered.

The practical things one can do about thinking include the following:

1. Be conscious of the process. You can think very effectively without knowing much about thinking. But if you are not satisfied with your thinking and want to improve it, you must pay some attention to it.

2. Spend some time on it. Most useful thinking is done outside special thinking sessions. On the whole, this ordinary thinking is a competent type of reaction thinking. Circumstances change, new information comes in, and one reacts appropriately. Planning, innovation, change often require some deliberate thinking time. The ideas themselves are certainly not confined to this thinking time, but it does provide the framework in which the ideas occur. It also takes the ideas and examines and develops them.

3. Develop attitudes. Attitudes are not techniques. Attitudes are general reactions. One attitude may encourage new ideas, change, exploration. Another attitude might look only for the immediate, the sound, and the practical. There may be a synthesis attitude, or an analytical one, or a creative one. None of them is exclusive but they are distinct. One can switch from one to the other, but there must be something to switch to.

4. Develop tools. Tools for thinking are tools for changing information around until it makes better sense. Mathematical techniques are thinking tools. So is language. Special operational words such as NO allow us to handle information in useful ways. Notation is another tool. So are visual display methods such as graphs. One can also use mechanical devices such as calculators or computers. In each case, the tools are independent of the actual information that is fed into them. The tools are artificial devices. One tool may be more appropriate in one setting than in another but as basic change devices they can be used anywhere.

5. Be aware of mistakes. Most of the time, one is seeking to change information around so that it can trigger an appropriate reaction pattern. This is where the main effort of thinking is concentrated. Yet the natural tendency of information is to trigger reaction patterns. Quite often these are inappropriate and sometimes consistently so. An important part of the process of thinking is to be aware of the possible errors.

6. Escape from inhibiting procedures. One may have developed attitudes or even procedures which, while useful in certain areas, can be restrictive in others. In order to improve one's thinking, one may have to realize the inhibitory effects of such tendencies and to escape from them. Simple escape is not easy unless one actually sets up an alternative procedure.

Lateral thinking

The general points about thinking apply as well to lateral thinking. In trying to improve the ability to think laterally, one does three things:
1. Develops an attitude toward change and toward new ideas.
2. Escapes from the inhibiting restrictions of vertical thinking.
3. Develops techniques and tools (including a new operational word).

These three things run into one another. In the following pages some of the techniques of lateral thinking are described. In reading about the techniques and in using them, one becomes aware of the lateral thinking attitude and of the restricting tendencies of vertical thinking. At the same time one learns a technique that can be used. Above all, the techniques provide a formal opportunity for the practice of lateral thinking until such time as it becomes an automatic skill. In particular, the new operational word PO serves as a crystallization of the attitudes and practice of lateral thinking.

Basic principles of lateral thinking 4

It may be useful at this point to outline the basic principles of lateral thinking. The concept of lateral thinking may be considered under three headings:

1. Background

The need for lateral thinking arises from the way the mind behaves as a patterning system which requires discontinuity in order to change patterns and bring them up to date.

2. Process

Lateral thinking is concerned with change—with the escape from old ideas and the generation of new ones.

3. Method

The use of lateral thinking consists in an awareness of the patterning nature of mind, an appreciation of the difference between the rules of vertical thinking and the rules of lateral thinking, the application of special settings or techniques and of a new operational word.

These three headings can be considered in a little more detail.

Background

- The mind acts to create patterns, to recognize patterns, and to use patterns, but not to change them.
- Sheer continuity is responsible for most ideas rather than a repeated assessment of their value.
- We have developed tools for establishing ideas and developing them but not for changing them.
- An idea *cannot* make the best use of available information (this is de Bono's First Law); an idea arises from the nature of a sequential patterning system.

- No way of looking at things can be the best possible one (this is another way of putting the preceding law).
- Thinking is not only a matter of using concepts but also of being able to change them.
- It is possible to change ideas by developing them but it may also be necessary to change them by restructuring them.
- The patterning system of mind needs the introduction of discontinuity in order to make the best use of available information.

Process

Lateral thinking involves two basic processes:

1. ESCAPE
2. PROVOCATION

These two basic processes may be considered separately:

Escape

- Recognition of dominant or polarizing ideas.
- The deliberate search for alternative ways of looking at things or doing things. The search is for alternative ways, not for the best way.
- Refusal to accept assumptions or to take things for granted.
- An attempt to escape from concept prisons: "dis-concepting" or "un-concepting."
- An attack on arrogance attached to *any* way of looking at things.
- The realization that beneath the current way of looking at things lie other alternative ways waiting to be discovered.
- The need to enlarge the problem context, to shift attention to other areas, to shift the entry point.
- Recognition of the danger of being blocked by openness (by adequate ideas that prevent the development of better ones).

Provocation

- The separation of the generation of ideas from their judgment or evaluation.
- Looking at an idea to see where it can lead to or what it can trigger off rather than to see if it is correct.

- The making of unjustified leaps and then catching up with them.
- It may be necessary to be wrong at some stage in order to reach the right solution.
- There may not be a reason for saying something until after it has been said. The justification for a change may be apparent only after the change has been made.
- You may have to be at the top of a mountain in order to find the best way up. When an idea has come about, hindsight analysis may fully justify it.
- The use of chance as a provocative source of discontinuity.
- Movement for the sake of movement in order to *generate* a direction instead of to *follow* one.

Method

This may be considered separately under three headings:

1. ATTITUDE
2. TECHNIQUES AND SKILL
3. NEW OPERATIONAL WORD

Attitude
- Awareness of the danger of being trapped by a fixed way of looking at things.
- Awareness of the danger of concept prisons.
- Awareness of the difference between the first and second stages of thinking.
- Awareness of the difference between lateral and vertical thinking.
- Awareness that adequacy does not preclude a better idea.
- Awareness of the need to look for different ways of doing things rather than being satisfied by the apparent best.
- Awareness of the dangers of arrogance and righteousness about a particular idea.
- Awareness of the need to use ideas in a practical manner and yet realize the need to change them.

Techniques and skill
- Techniques are formal settings which encourage the use of lateral thinking.
- Techniques can be learned and used even if one does not accept the principles on which they are based.

● Techniques are useful only insofar as they are useful. To begin with there is the matter of learning the technique and practicing it until one can use it with skill and confidence. But if it does not prove useful, choose another one. Individual preferences vary.

● Apart from their deliberate use, techniques are valuable as settings in which to practice the habit of lateral thinking so that eventually it becomes a natural part of thinking and is no longer confined to a "technique" situation.

● Skill in lateral thinking depends on natural ability, on an understanding of the processes involved, on the ability to overcome the educated inhibitions of vertical thinking, and on the practice of lateral thinking to the point of confidence.

● Skill takes time to develop. A continued gentle effort is more effective than sudden bouts of fierce effort.

● The ability to think laterally may actually be most valuable when it is not applied deliberately but as a natural acquired habit of thought without conscious effort.

● Even if one never uses any techniques and never develops any skill in lateral thinking, an awareness of the principles can make it easier to understand the dangers of fixed ideas and the need to develop new ones. Such an awareness can also make it easier to get on with people who are concerned with developing new ideas.

New operational word

● A new operational word (PO) serves as a tool for lateral thinking.

● PO bears the same relationship to lateral thinking that NO does to logical thinking.

The use of PO is described in Chapter 13.

Summary

The purpose of lateral thinking is the generation of new ideas and the escape from old ones. The need for lateral thinking arises from the patterning behavior of mind which is not good at restructuring ideas to bring them up to date and allow full use of available information. The traditional habits of thinking are very effective at developing ideas but not very good at restructuring them. Lateral thinking is designed to supplement traditional thinking, and especially to introduce the discontinuity that is necessary for restructuring ideas. The basic process of lateral thinking is the escape from old ideas and the provocation of new ones. The ideas generated by lateral thinking are selected and developed by traditional thinking methods. A new functional word is introduced as the basic tool of lateral thinking.

The principles of lateral thinking could be summarized as follows:

1. Recognition of dominant or polarizing ideas
2. The search for different ways of looking at things
3. A relaxation of the rigid control of vertical thinking
4. The use of chance and provocative methods in order to introduce discontinuity
5. An understanding of the new operational word PO and some skill in its use

Lateral thinking techniques. Group I: Recognizing current ideas

Before setting out to generate new ideas or to escape from the old ones, it is well to be aware of the current ideas. It is not so much a matter of defining them in order to try to avoid them, but simply of defining them in a *clear manner*. The effort of defining them can itself show up the fixity of the ideas. Once the ideas have been recognized, then one moves naturally to ways of changing them or escaping from them. The following list suggests some headings which can be used in examining current ideas. The headings are but different aspects of ideas. They are not in any way exclusive, and it would be possible to generate other headings.

1. DOMINANT IDEAS
2. TETHERING FACTORS (OR CRUCIAL FACTORS)
3. POLARIZING TENDENCIES
4. BOUNDARIES
5. ASSUMPTIONS

1. Dominant ideas

● A dominant idea organizes the approach to a problem or situation just as a dominant person might organize a group.

● A dominant idea may be stated explicitly but more often there is only a general awareness of the idea. For instance, a group may be dominated by the idea of the best return on capital investment and so come to consider various schemes and the returns. Dominated by this idea, the group would be unable to plan for flexibility which involves not some definite return but being in a position to make the best use of changing circumstances.

● A dominant idea may be inherited along with the situation itself, or may be part of the way the situation is traditionally handled. For instance, an advertising agency may be dominated by the idea that the same theme has to be carried through in the various media.

● A dominant idea does not refer to the problem situation itself but to *the way it is looked at*. This point is illustrated in Figure 5–1. Many people think that the search for the dominant idea is the search for the essence of the problem. It is nothing of the sort. It is a search for the way the problem is being looked at. You may set out to find the dominant idea in your own thinking, or in the thinking of your group, or in the thinking of someone else, or in a written report. Once you have identified the dominant idea, you should be in a position to tell how the problem will continue to be approached.

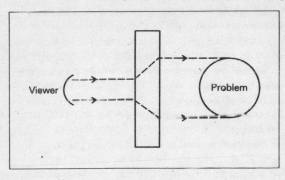

**Figure 5–1.
The way the
problem is looked at**

● It is easy to have a vague notion of the dominant idea. But this is not good enough. One should be able to identify it clearly enough to be able to write it down. And until one becomes good at identifying dominant ideas one should actually write them down on each occasion. There is an optimum way of expressing the dominant idea. Too many words will make it too detailed and too few words will make it so general that it is useless. For instance, in discussing supermarket organization someone's thinking may be dominated by an idea which could be expressed in the following three ways:

Concerned with laying out the display shelves and check-out counters to ensure that the customers can move around easily, can find what they want, and are not delayed at the check-out point.

Customers' convenience.

The customer.

The last expression is too vague to be much use because

it could refer to attracting customers, market research, siting of stores, and the like.

- In a written report it is useful to try to underline the phrase or sentence which best expresses the dominant idea.
- When different people set out to find the dominant idea they usually come up with different answers and then start arguing as to which is the *real* dominant idea. Obviously, some people are more skilled at picking out the dominant idea than others. Some of the ideas turned up will also be more dominant than others. Nevertheless, there is no such thing as *the* dominant idea. One person may perceive one dominant idea and another person may perceive another. Even the person doing the thinking may believe himself to be dominated by one idea; yet someone else may quite rightly maintain that the person is dominated by a different idea. The main point is the effort to find the dominant idea. This is what matters. *On the route* to this destination, one turns up a great many ideas which are organizing the way the problem is being treated.
- In any situation there may be more than one dominant idea. For instance, in considering the problem of teacher shortage one may be dominated by the idea that teaching is a vocation. One may also be dominated by the idea that teachers are an essential part of the presentation of knowledge to students. One may also be dominated by the idea that the more teachers there are, the better the education.
- It may be quite difficult to recognize the idea that is dominating one's own thinking, but it is worth making the effort until one is good at it. As a check (or in the first place) you can always ask someone else to identify for you the idea dominating your approach to a problem.

2. Tethering factors (or crucial factors)

- A dominant idea is a powerful organizing idea, but a tethering factor may be a small, almost insignificant idea. Usually the tethering factor is unrecognized as such and often it is overlooked completely. A tethering factor is that factor which is always included in any solution or approach to that particular problem. It is assumed that this factor has to be included. For instance, it is assumed that a person should pay more if he uses more of a service provided for him. This would mean that in a car park the charge would increase with the length of time the car stayed there. And yet one can imagine a situation in which the longer a car stayed in a park the less it would cost—this would help get commuters' cars off the streets, so leaving them to shoppers. Similarly, a person in a shopping area who left his car all morning would be doing the stores more good (since he might be expected to be shopping all this time) than a person who parked only for the half-hour required to make a single purchase.

● The trouble with tethering factors is that they never come up for examination. They do not control the solution as much as dominant ideas but they do restrict mobility. For instance, in an advertising campaign it may be taken for granted that the ads should run for a month. Attention is focused on the ads themselves and on the media to be chosen. This tethering factor of the month is left unexamined. If it were to be examined, it might be seen that the only reason behind it was that the accounts department found it easier to work in months. Yet, from a promotion point of view, two weeks separated by two weeks might have been far more effective.

● Often there is difficulty in distinguishing between a dominant idea and a tethering factor. It does not really matter what you call it so long as it is recognized. On the whole a dominant idea is more pervasive and more important than a tethering factor.

● It is not so much a matter of examining the tethering factor to see if it is justified but of realizing that one's freedom of movement in finding a solution is restricted by it. Whether the tethering factor can be dropped or not, it still remains a tethering factor.

● In any situation, there may be one or several tethering factors—or even a whole list.

3. Polarizing tendencies

● A polarizing tendency involves the creation of an either/ or situation. Instead of the rigidity of a fixed idea, one has definite mobility but a mobility *only* between two defined opposites. In a way, polarizing tendencies are more restricting than dominant ideas or tethering factors because they give an illusion of freedom, of choice, and of the consideration of alternatives. Polarizing tendencies are especially restricting in bargaining and labor relations. By setting up two firm positions in advance, one inevitably finds oneself in one of them in the end.

● A polarizing tendency may be detected in two opposite ways of looking at a situation: for instance, medical care is either a commodity or a social right. Or a polarizing tendency may be used to define a position rigidly by showing what it is not. Thus, a research manager may stress that his researchers should either work in an academic community and be free to follow their own ideas, or be paid out of company money and so follow the company's requirements. In fact, some freedom to follow one's own creative interests does the company as much good as it does the researcher.

● The existence of polarizing extremes makes it impossible to hold an intermediate position. There is an obvious danger of this in the assessment of personnel for promotion. Faults and virtues become fixed at extreme ends of the scale because that makes decision easier.

● The important point is to be able to recognize a polarizing tendency when it disguises itself as flexibility but actually shuts out alternatives. For instance, in considering the site of a new airport it might be held that there are only two possibilities: to satisfy the requirements of the airport users or to satisfy the requirements of the environment.

● A polarizing tendency does not only refer to two fixed alternatives. It refers to any number of fixed alternatives which are presented as the only possible ways of looking at the problem.

4. Boundaries

● Boundaries are limiting conditions. Boundaries are the framework within which a problem is supposed to be considered.

● Usually one looks in from the boundaries toward the problem and takes for granted that it exists within certain boundaries. But it can be useful to look outward at these boundaries and to consider what they really are.

● Problems are never completely open-ended. There is

always a set of conditions which have to be met. There is always a set of circumstances within which one is expected to work. These constitute the boundaries. They may be carefully laid down as in a design specification. Or they may be so vague that one only becomes aware of them when one runs up against them and is told that things cannot be done that way.

● When the boundaries are vague or undefined it is useful to find out what they are. But even when they are well defined, it is useful to make oneself conscious of them— not for the purpose of keeping within them but so that one can question whether a particular requirement really is necessary. For instance, in the running of a railway it is taken for granted that the shipper is allowed a considerable time at each end of the journey for loading and unloading. A reduction in the time spent in this free warehousing would allow a better utilization of rolling stock.

● In certain areas, such as marketing, a whole mythology develops based on past experience. Aspects of such mythologies constitute very definite boundaries to the way specific problem situations are viewed. Such myths are not necessarily false, but a definite awareness of their influence is necessary.

● Quite often a novel solution to a problem is regarded as cheating because it ignores certain boundaries which everyone else had accepted. The very cry of "cheating" indicates the absolute nature of the boundaries. This attitude is reasonable enough where the boundaries are legal but too often it is carried over into quite different situations.

● The design of a new product is often surrounded by boundaries which are derived partly from preconceptions of what the product should be and partly from the performance of other products in the past. Such boundaries prevent the free development of a *new* product and, in the end, allow only a minor variation on an old product. It is not a matter of doing without specifications but of being aware of those actually used, and also of the fact that specifications need not always precede development but can, in part, follow along with it. That is to say, the advantages of a new product once it has developed can be considerable and cannot always have been laid down as specifications beforehand.

5. Assumptions

● No matter how far back one goes in one's thinking, the starting point is always based on a set of assumptions. If one were not to use assumptions, one would never be able to think at all.

● Whereas boundaries are the limits which restrict the free growth of an idea, assumptions are the material that is fed in to make the idea grow.

● Some assumptions are valid, some assumptions are invalid, some assumptions may be usefully treated as valid even if they are not.

● The first point is not to examine the validity of an assumption but to be aware that it is being made. In one's own thinking, or in listening to the thinking of others, one can pause and outline an assumption by saying: "We are here assuming that . . .".

● Assumptions can vary a great deal in their acceptability. It is an assumption that employees require payment. It is also an assumption that employees will work harder for more money. The first assumption is not unchallengeable although it seems more like a fact. But to treat the second one as a fact excludes such factors as job satisfaction, motivation, job security, and even the consideration that unusually high wages might attract unproductive employees.

● Block assumptions are often made up of other assumptions which vary in their validity. That an increase in fares will reduce passenger traffic on a carrier is an assumption which might be made together with the assumption that a reduction in fares will increase passenger traffic, to give a block assumption about the relationship of fares to traffic. Another way this can happen is by extrapolation from one assumption to another. It is an assumption to suppose that because holiday bookings in one place have fallen off markedly they will fall off equally in other places.

● The danger with assumptions is not simply that they may be used when they are invalid. To some extent this is the sort of risk one *has* to take if one is going to think at all. The danger is that they *escape attention*. In a takeover bid or merger situation, it is easy to assume that the other company's profits are calculated on a similar basis to one's own. Yet, in a situation like a franchising business, the accounting practice may be very different indeed.

● The trouble is that once one starts trying to look at assumptions the process is never ending. One can get so confused with uncertainty and doubt as assumption piles on assumption that one may prefer to go ahead without such an examination. For instance, it is an assumption that the world demand for nickel will increase. It is also an assumption that the price will remain high. It is an assumption that present mines and new mines will do no more than meet the demand—without overproduction. But all this rests on the assumption that the nickel-extracting process remains the same. Yet new methods of extracting nickel from low-grade laterite ores can change the whole picture.

● It is never possible or practical to examine all assumptions. In setting out to look at assumptions, one is not trying to look at all of them. One is trying to become *aware* of some of them. The aim is not an analysis of the situation. The aim is to become aware of some assumptions in order to set off some new ideas.

Lateral thinking techniques. Group II: Changing ideas by avoidance

6

The preceding section dealt with the recognition of current ideas. The purpose was to make visible those ideas which were directing the approach to a problem situation. There was no question of trying to change these ideas or challenge them. Identification was all that was required. This is an important point because unless one separates identification from challenge or alteration there is a tendency to *avoid* identifying those ideas which one is reluctant to alter.

Simple recognition of a current idea can do much to free one from its domination. Very often it is not the idea itself which is difficult to escape from but the hidden nature of an idea which exists only as a vague awareness. This may happen with one's own ideas or more especially with the ideas of others. With regard to the ideas of others, it does not matter if the person concerned refuses to recognize a certain idea as dominating his thinking. So long as you recognize it, you can better appreciate what is going on and why there may be difficulty in generating or accepting new ideas.

The step from recognition of an idea to avoiding that idea is a small one. It should, however, be a deliberate step. One should be able to recognize an idea without at once trying to avoid it. It is only if one wants to make the next step that one tries to avoid the idea that has been recognized. "Avoidance" is a general term and refers not so much to avoiding the idea itself but avoiding its tendency to dominate, tether, polarize, restrict, et cetera.

Avoidance devices

There is no need to learn special avoidance techniques, for the avoidance attitude is all that is required. This can be expressed in quite ordinary language:

Let's forget about that for the moment.

Is there another way of looking at this?

What would happen if we did not make that assumption?
Aren't we being dominated by this idea?
Are these the only alternatives?
Do we have to take either of these positions?
If we were not restricted by that consideration, what would
we do?
That is probably true but let us suppose it is just a myth.
We'll come back to that point but let's try some other
ideas first.
Is that so important?
Is that as essential as everyone always believes?

Lateral thinking is not specifically concerned with problem
analysis. For that reason, the challenging of assumptions and
attempts to prove them invalid are not themselves part of
the lateral thinking process. Lateral thinking is not concerned with proving an assumption or an idea inadequate
and so moving on to a better one. Lateral thinking is concerned with moving on to a *different* idea, whether or not
the assumption is valid. The aim is to generate different ideas
and to escape from the old ones *not to prove or disprove the
old ones*. In any case, one would quite often find the old
ideas quite justified because one would be looking at them
through the old frame of reference. Thus, if you were looking
for a way to make a hole, you would find a drill an excellent
tool. But this is because our notion of a hole is already
conditioned to the type that is máde by a drill. In fact, for
many purposes, square holes might be better.

Question

A child asks "why" all the time not so much because he is
looking for explanations but because he wants a phenomenon
explained in terms he understands so that he can link it up
with other things. Behind the use of the word "why" is the
effort to expand an idea so that one can see what is behind
it. "Why" can be used as a challenge in order to get someone
to justify an idea he holds, but this may not be very useful
because it puts him on the defensive. As he rationalizes his
reasons for holding the idea, that idea becomes increasingly
rigid. But if "why" is used as a tool to *open up* an idea in an
exploratory fashion, it can be very useful. In fact, this particular use of "why" has been developed into a tool for
generating new ideas and many people find it useful.

Although the simple repeated use of "why" seems

straightforward enough there are some points to bear in mind.

- It is not much use being aggressive.
- If the other person finds difficulty in answering "why" at any point, he can be helped along with, "Is it because . . . ?"
- "Why" can be applied to the entire statement that has been made, but this leaves the other person the option of choosing what part of the statement to explain.

"The most important point in running a hotel is to keep the occupancy rate above 60 percent."
"Why?"
"Because the highest part of the takings comes from room rental."
"Why?"
"Because that is what a hotel is for. Other services are only subsidiary: 53 percent comes from rooms, 29 percent from food, 11 percent from drinks."

Instead of this total use of "why" it could have been focused more precisely on some part of the answer to the preceding "why."

"The most important point in running a hotel is to keep the occupancy rate above 60 percent."
"Why do you use that figure?"
"Because overheads are covered by this rate of occupancy and above it the takings are almost sheer profit."
"Why are overheads only covered at this figure?"
"Because fixed items like staff and kitchen facilities cannot be varied according to demand."
"Why can't they be varied?"
"Because in the case of the staff you could never keep them except on the basis of full employment."

From this point, one could then take off to consider methods whereby the guests could serve themselves, methods of rotating staff, utilizing their capacity more fully, and so on.

- The danger in the repeated use of "why" is that once you are set on a particular line, this line is developed and alternative lines are neglected. For instance, in the last example, ideas on how to keep occupancy above the 60 percent rate would not have been considered.
- The repeated use of "why" is often most useful when on is challenging a particular way of doing something rather

than generating ideas in a wide-open situation. An
established process or method can be shown to be no
more than an acquired habit.

● Some people find that the simple use of "why" generates
antagonism. They prefer to use some other formula such
as: "But for what? Would you be able to increase your
profits?" and so on. This formula changes the situation
from that of a person defending his ideas to a person
who is able to pick out the factor which is responsible
for those ideas.

Rotation of attention

The natural tendency is to find the core of a problem and to
focus attention on this. Training encourages this tendency.
Even apart from any active tendency to seek the core of a
problem, the natural way a problem presents itself suggests a
central field of attention. The deliberate rotation of attention
involves moving attention from its natural position at the
center of the problem to other parts of the situation. The
difficulty with doing this is twofold. The first difficulty is that
it seems pointless and a waste of time because one has been
trained to consider only the important things and to throw
out the rest. This is an attitude difficulty and can be overcome. The second difficulty is that one may not be able to
think of the various areas of attention that one should be
considering in rotation.

For instance, when a man is moved from one department
to manage another there are many aspects of the move
which could be called attention areas:

● The effect on the department he moves from.
● The effect on the department he moves to.
● The effect on the man himself.
● The effect on another man who expected to get the job
and did not.

These are all fairly obvious and it should not be difficult to
rotate attention through these areas. Even so, one might tend
to neglect the fact that no matter how suited the man may
be to the new job, the move precludes the use of his abilities
in a different job—perhaps one that has not yet been created.

It is easy enough to consider whether a particular line of
action has a worthwhile return, but not so easy to consider
what other activity the time and effort might have been spent
on. It is easy enough to consider the cost of a service, but

not so easy to consider the cost of doing without it. It is easy enough to consider the worth of an executive, but not so easy to consider the total cost of replacing him. It is easy enough to consider the number of people involved in producing a service, but not so easy to consider the minimal contraction of service that would reduce the number of people substantially. It is easy enough to consider the most efficient way to carry out a process, but not so easy to consider the most efficient way to produce waste. Yet there are instances where the waste product or the know-how acquired in dealing with it have proved more valuable than the product itself.

● In rotating attention over the different aspects of a problem the tendency is to pick out products, processes, or people involved. But relationships and time are just as much parts of the problem, even though they do not exist on their own. For instance, in the motor insurance area the eventual settlement of a claim may be all that matters to the insurance company but, to the person involved, the weeks, months, or even years before the claim is settled are very real. Attention to this area would give rise to such ideas as the no-fault insurance system. Similarly, the sequence wage claim–productivity bargain is itself an area of attention and one could reverse the sequence by suggesting that a productivity increase should automatically be matched by a wage rise.

● It can be useful to rotate attention over areas which are not there. A divergence from expectancy can be a significant attention area. What is not said can be as significant as what is said. Rotating attention is not a matter of reading hidden meanings into everything but of selecting attention areas outside the obvious ones.

● Finding the different areas of attention is not a matter of taking the situation and analyzing it into its parts, for such an analysis can leave out several attention areas which may be not different things but different ways of looking at the same thing. For instance, in considering unemployment it is easy enough to divide the problem into size and distribution of labor force, mobility, skills, et cetera, but easy to leave out of consideration the turn-around pool which includes those leaving one job and looking around for a better one.

● There is probably no such thing as a complete rotation of attention because no matter how hard one tries, attention glides to those areas which already have enough meaning to exist as areas.

Change of entry point

In a patterning system the point at which one enters a pattern is of the most fundamental importance. This is because it is one of the few ways one has of working through existing patterns and yet coming up with a different answer. This point is discussed in greater detail in a later section. For the moment it is enough to consider that thinking is a sequential process and that one actually starts off at some point. By changing around that point, one may be able to look at a situation in a new way.

● Changing the entry point is not a matter of listing all possible entry points and then going through them all or picking out the most promising. It is simply a matter of *changing the entry point*. That is to say, one acknowledges the usual entry point and deliberately shifts to some other entry point.

● There is no question of judging the usefulness of an entry point before using it. To do so would mean judging it in terms of the current way of looking at the problem, and hence an entry point chosen in this way would be unlikely to throw up new ideas.

● Changing the entry point may be a matter of looking around for another entry point at the beginning or it may mean choosing an entry point somewhere along the line of development of the problem. The difference between the two is shown in Figure 6–1. The difficulty in choosing an entry point somewhere along the line of thinking about the problem is that one may not know what that line is until it has developed. This is not always the case, for one usually tries lateral thinking after one has tried vertical thinking. In this case, one simply chooses an entry point somewhere along the line of thinking that has been used.

● Quite a common way of changing the entry point is to jump to the endpoint of a problem and work backward. With many problems, the endpoint is clearly defined and the problem is one of getting there. In such cases it may be easier to work backward. If you work forward, you can never be certain that a particular line of thought is going to get you anywhere near the solution.

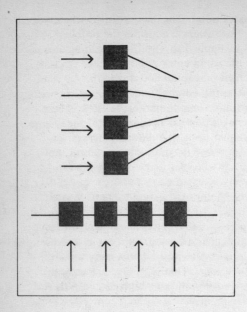

Figure 6–1.

But if you work backward, you can be absolutely sure that your line of thought is going to end up at the solution. Once you have developed a sound path from the starting point to the solution it cannot possibly matter from which end you have constructed it.

● A different entry point can give quite different results. In considering the traffic congestion in London, the planners at one time took street-parked cars as their entry point. They ended up with regulations that required each new office building to have adequate car park facilities attached to it. Later on they shifted, or were forced to shift, their entry point to the cars actually moving in and out of the city along the roads. From this new entry point, it was at once obvious that providing every building with a car park only increased the problem by encouraging the people in the building to travel in and out by car. So the regulations were changed round again.

● How precise is an entry point? It may be an idea, it may be a situation at one point in time, or it may be an aspect of something. The entry point need not even be a single idea. Once again, the aim is not to find the best entry point. Nor is it to refine an entry point. Nor is it to analyze an entry point. The entry point is where your thinking starts. For instance, consider the problem of the charge that can be applied to a toll road leading into a city: one could use as an entry point the need to establish a certain return on capital and divide this by road usage to arrive at a toll charge; one could use as an entry point the charge made on comparable toll roads; one could use as an entry point the estimation of the charge that the traffic would bear, calculating the effect on traffic density of a progressive increase in charge, and using that charge at which traffic density started to decline; one could use as an entry point the minimal charge that could be imposed without deterring traffic since the road may be supposed to be a public service in the first place; or one could use as an entry point the passenger value of the road as opposed to the car value. This last entry point could lead to such ideas as a toll charge on the empty seats in a car. Thus a nominal four-seater car with only one passenger would pay four times as much as a four-seater car with four passengers. Both from a revenue point of view and also from a public service point of view, this might be a good idea. In this case the entry point is a fairly complex one. It could be described as the "utility" of the road, but this is a bit too general. It is closer to the idea of a road as a public service to move the largest amount of people around with the greatest convenience.

● Although one is not trying to discover all possible entry points or even the best one, it may be useful to list a few alternative entry points before moving ahead to explore any particular one. There is no question of making an exhaustive list. But the exercise of generating new entry points is itself valuable quite apart from the pursuit of any particular one.

Quota of alternatives

Lateral thinking is all about escaping from fixed ways of looking at things and generating new ways. The very word lateral suggests not the development of an idea but the sideways move to generate parallel ideas, alternative approaches. It may seem that the lateral search for alternatives is what one naturally does in a situation anyway. There are, however, points of difference:

1. The natural search for alternatives is directed to finding the best approach. In lateral thinking, however, one is not looking for the *best* approach but for *other* approaches. The emphasis is on novelty and difference, not on suitability.
2. The natural search for alternatives takes place only when the obvious approach is seen to be inadequate or when there is no obvious approach. The lateral search for alternatives takes place even when there is an obvious approach which seems highly satisfactory.
3. The alternatives considered in the natural search are the reasonable ones which fit in with the general idea of the problem. The alternatives considered in the lateral search may at first sight appear to be quite unreasonable.

● The point about the lateral search for alternatives is that it must be deliberate and, to begin with, it needs to be *artificial*.

● One sets up an artificial QUOTA which gives the number of alternative ways of looking at the situation which must be filled. Such a QUOTA may be 3, 4, 5.

● There is no point in using a larger QUOTA than 5 even if one does want to show off one's lateral ability. Setting too large a QUOTA is discouraging because it becomes difficult to fill on *every occasion* and so one does not develop a QUOTA habit. All that happens is that the situations which are easy to approach in different ways get treated in this manner (and they probably do not need it) but the situations which really do need it are regarded as being immune to the treatment. It is far better to have a small QUOTA which it is possible to fill on each occasion. Another disadvantage of having a large QUOTA is that one tends to fill it with subtle variations on the same idea. With a small QUOTA, the alternatives can be as different as possible. They can also serve as main headings which are then broken down into variations.

● With the QUOTA system the emphasis is on the differences between the alternatives rather than on their number.

● The artificiality of the QUOTA system is necessary to ensure that, if one does come across a very promising approach, one can put it aside for the moment and proceed with the task of filling the QUOTA.

Without some such task, the temptation is to pursue the

promising approach as soon as one finds it—even if it is the first alternative considered.

- It is best to list the alternatives on a piece of paper because trying to remember them all prevents one going on to a new idea. Also, when one has them written down it may be apparent that a new alternative is not really so different after all.

- In filling a QUOTA, one may easily end up by listing different *aspects* of a problem which are not really different approaches. There is no definite way of avoiding this. It is usually enough to be conscious of the danger. The other safeguard is to consider the quality of the alternatives. If all of them seem very sound and sensible, then one may not be generating alternatives at all but simply analyzing a problem into its different aspects. To some extent one should be "surprised" by the alternative approach which one turns up.

- There is no question of there being "correct" alternatives which one should arrive at. There is no question of arguing in a group situation that some alternatives are right and others are not. Nor is there really much point in arguing that another person's alternatives are not as separate as your own. This may become obvious to him when you tell him yours. Or you can ask the other person to elaborate on his approaches to see if they really are different when they are pursued a little way.

- What happens when one has generated these alternative approaches? One can follow all of them or any one of them as far as one wishes. But there is no question of analyzing each one to see where it would lead or whether it would be useful. The exercise is to generate the alternatives. The purpose of this is to free one from the idea that there is only one possible point of view. Merely generating the alternatives can provide a new insight into the problem. In practice the things that can happen may be listed as follows:

1. Escape from the rigidity of one way of looking at the problem.
2. Generate new ideas even if no new approach is followed up.
3. The discovery of a new approach which is itself worth following up.
4. Return to the first idea or the most promising approach but no longer because it is the only one that was thought of.

5. One of the alternative approaches, though useless in itself, can trigger a useful new approach.
6. By generating alternatives, one becomes more ready to appreciate and understand the differing viewpoints of others.

● Quite often the alternative approaches may actually seem like solutions or at least solution areas. Consider the problem of a business which requires highly trained operators (for instance, telephone operators). After an expensive training during which they do not do much work but are paid a salary, the operators leave with their new qualifications and find more lucrative work with a business which has not paid anything toward their training. This problem could be looked at in such ways as the following:

1. Take only trained people; do not train at all.
2. Subsidize job training in this field as part of general education having nothing to do with the business itself. Or provide a direct (perhaps government subsidized) educational service.
3. Simplify system so that training is not so complex and costly.
4. Step up useful work that can be done during training (in the same or related areas) so that even if operators leave they will have contributed something.
5. Negotiate contracts which call for a minimum period of service after training.
6. Charge for training by deduction from salary with repayment during service years.
7. Provide salary and job structure so that there is no incentive to leave.

Some of these (for instance, 5 and 6) can be combined. All of them are approaches to the solution of the problem. If one were trying to find alternative ways of *describing* the problem, alternatives such as the following might have been used:

1. We don't have the trained people we need and we cannot get them.
2. We don't recover the money we spend on training.
3. We are providing a community educational service.
4. We are subsidizing other businesses by doing their training for them.

It does not matter whether one generates problem description alternatives or solution area alternatives. Someone else might choose to generate alternatives as follows:

1. The problem is that training is so expensive.
2. The problem is that we cannot operate without trained people.
3. The problem is that the trained people leave us.
4. The problem is that we cannot leave the training to anyone else because no one else is doing it.

All these alternatives are very reasonable and many of them are but different ways of saying the same thing. This does not matter. As has been repeated again and again, the most important thing is the *effort* to find different ways of looking at things. The effort eventually becomes a habit and an attitude. Even if it never turns up any useful alternatives, it will at least have diminished the arrogance with which fixed points of view are held.

Concept changing

The first aspect of lateral thinking is the avoiding of fixed ways of looking at things. This may mean deliberately avoiding fixed concepts. Concepts may not themselves be actual ways of looking at things, but they do strongly influence these ways. For the purpose of this section, it is assumed that a single concept is capable of being expressed by a single word. Thus one might have such concepts as "productivity," "retail," "investment," "brand image," and the like. In the consideration of a situation, those concepts which are basic to the situation occur again and again, and it is taken for granted that one has no choice but to deal with them. If one makes an effort to avoid the standard concept and expresses this effort as the choice of another word or concept, then it becomes easier to escape from the old way of looking at things.

The area in which concept changing has the most striking effect is the legal area. Laws are set up to deal not with things but with concepts. A law which forbids a certain concept becomes inoperative if that concept is changed. When conglomerates were showing what could be done by attention to the management of assets, the banks wished to enter the same field but were barred by law from diversification of this sort. Their answer was to change the concept of their operation by establishing a one-bank holding company which was free to make acquisitions. Like Canada, Mexico has an overland exemption from the oil quota restrictions on importing oil into the USA. But there is no overland pipeline from Mexico, so the oil is shipped in tankers to Brownsville, put into trucks, and sent back across the border into Mexico, whereupon the trucks turn round and come back "importing oil overland into the USA". Federal Reserve Board regulations require that a secured loan should be backed by listed securities equal to five times the value of the loan as collateral. This became a problem when Kirk Kerkorian wished to raise money to acquire MGM. The problem was overcome by a simple change of concept. The bank advanced him money as an unsecured loan. In hedge funds, the managers of the funds improved their tax position by becoming partners. In the United States, one-third of all new single family dwellings are mobile homes. There are various reasons for this, but there is also the basic change of concept since a mobile home is regarded as a vehicle rather than a building and so it is not subject to building codes, union restrictions, or real estate tax.

The legal area is an artificial situation where a change of concept allows one to proceed in an entirely different way. The same thing holds equally well outside the legal area, though its effect may be less clear cut. If one's choice of action is restricted by the concepts through which one looks at the environment, then a change in such concepts can mean a greater freedom of action. The concept of "ownership" means that a business has a lot of capital tied up in its factories. One way of escaping this is to sell the factories and then lease back, so freeing working capital. The franchise business is an escape from the concept of "ownership" as well. Here the services, goodwill, advertising, and so on, are divorced from the actual ownership of stock or premises.

Un-concepting

"Un-concepting" or "dis-concepting" are ugly words, intended only to imply the reversal of the process by which concepts are formed. Different bits of experience come together to give an overall concept which covers the whole situation. These concepts themselves come together to give a further concept. And so the process goes on in a hierarchical manner until in the end one is dealing with apparently simple concepts, each of which describes the situation in a comprehensive but fixed way. Thus the huge concepts of totalitarianism or democracy apparently refer to quite small aspects of a government situation, but in fact they refer to large organizations as they exist at the moment. Unconcepting implies an attempt to break down the concepts so that one can better see what is behind them and even try to look at it in a different way.

Dropping a concept

The simplest way to change the effect a concept has on a situation is to avoid that concept by dropping it from the discussion. Thus if the concept "profits" was dominating a discussion, one would continue the discussion without that word. In practice it would simply mean that no one was allowed to say the word "profits". Those taking part in the discussion would find roundabout ways of saying the same thing. But in using these roundabout ways one can more easily come up with fresh ideas. Thus the expressions, "payment for services", "payment for risk", "forward upkeep of an establishment to provide a service", "advance payment for change", could all lead to more ideas than the simple word "profit". For instance, one might come up with the idea that profit was just a *time* device to allow a change to come about in the future ahead of the absolute necessity for that change. For instance, profits in the drugs industry allow and make worthwhile drug research ahead of demand. Profits in the airlines industry allow the acquisition of new generations of jetliners. In other words, profits can be looked upon as time devices not just as reward devices.

In discussing the labor situation one might try dropping the concept "productivity". One would then be forced to use such phrases as "size of labor force related to value of output", or "effect of each worker on the ongoing production process". From such phrases, one could come up with ideas like the distribution of productivity; sensitive points where a small change would markedly affect productivity elsewhere; and developing means for dealing with such points rather than overall productivity incentives. It may be more a matter of reorganization than incentives. Similarly one could come up with the idea that increased productivity required not more effort but the willingness of workers to provide less effort and accept the introduction of machines to magnify their own efforts. These are all simple and obvious ideas but they arise more easily when one decides to drop the overall concept "productivity".

Fractionation

Fractionation means dividing a concept into parts. Fractionation is *not* an analysis. An analysis would involve breaking a concept down into its component parts. Such an analysis is a justifiable procedure in its own right, but it is not part of lateral thinking. The limitation of a true analysis is that the parts obtained are the very ones which have already come together to give the overall concept, and they will tend to do so again. In fractionation one divides up an overall concept into any parts whatsoever. The aim of the procedure is simply to escape from the concept itself. It does not matter so much where one has escaped to, as long as one has escaped.

Fractionation may involve breaking down the concept into several parts or breaking it down into two parts. The latter is far simpler to do. The basic procedure is to extract some idea from the overall concept and then see what is left. Having extracted one part from the concept, one then forms the remainder into the second part. Thus one does not actually have to search for two constituent parts. Often it is the effort to form the remainder into a coherent idea that sets off a new way of looking at things.

One could take the problem of air fares. In 1970 airlines were having a hard time because the projected 14 percent increase in traffic turned out to be no higher than 7 percent. This meant that the expensive Jumbojets provided over-capacity and passenger loads fell from 58 to 50 percent. Furthermore, the hoped-for reduction in unit operating cost with the new jets was less than anticipated because of spiralling costs (12 to 15 percent instead of 20 to 40 percent). The big jets had of course to be paid for. The problem involved the raising of air fares in the face of a demand which was not increasing and which might be discouraged by higher fares.

The first obvious split of the "air fare" concept would be into "attractiveness to passengers" and "profitability". If one now takes "attractiveness to passengers" one can extract from it "used advantage", and one is then left with "apparent advantage". The difference is that "used advantage" refers to actual passenger needs and is enjoyed by those who are already flying. "Apparent advantage" creates the envelope of attractiveness within which demand can grow. "Apparent advantage" can be offset against a fare increase more readily than "used advantage".

74

For instance, airlines could expand into the total travel package with hotel accommodation and surface self-drive car rental as an integral booking. Another idea would be to give "repeater" advantages. Thus every flight would give a 25 percent fare reduction on a further flight made with the same airline within a year. This would mean that every fifth flight within a year would be free. The same principle could make every third journey within a year a first-class journey.

As with other lateral thinking procedures, there is no question of finding the *right* way to divide up a concept. It is a matter of producing change; of avoiding the way one was looking at the situation before. Change is what matters, not rightness. The usefulness of an idea is assessed after an idea has come about, not before.

Fractionation trees

This is just an extension of the fractionation procedure. Instead of being content to divide a concept into parts, one then takes each of these parts and divides it again. One can go on in this manner as long as one likes until one has a treelike structure, the trunk being formed by the original concept and the twigs by the ultimate subdivision parts. As before, the procedure is *not* one of analysis. In this case it can very easily end up as an analysis. For instance, considering the problem of the use of credit in stores. At each stage there is a division into two parts.

Credit:
1. Volume of use of credit.
2. Reliability, that is, eventual payment of debt.
Volume of use:
1. Optional, a matter of convenience, goods could have been paid for in cash.
2. Compulsory; the purchase would not have been made in that store if there were no credit facilities.
Optional:
1. Larger volume of purchases at any one time, if these were not limited by immediate availability of cash.
2. Impulse buying, unplanned buying when no cash had been especially made ready.
Compulsory:
1. Avoidance of a store with no credit facilities.
2. Nondeliberate use of stores with credit facilities.

Or taking the other main branch:

Reliability:
1. Deliberate fraud.
2. Delay in payment.

Deliberate fraud:
1. Occasional.
2. Systematic.

Delay in payment:
1. Uniform delay in payment across all accounts.
2. Exceptional delay or infinite delay in some cases.

This particular tree is pretty close to an analysis except that there is no attempt to be comprehensive. From the same starting point, one might have branched off in a rather different way:

Credit:
1. Commitment by opportunity to a particular store.
2. Customers' use of a store's capital.

Or again:

Credit:
1. A time change convenience for the customer.
2. A time change inconvenience for the store.

Or again:

Credit:
1. Use of total purchasing ability as against immediate purchasing ability.
2. The selling not only of goods but of a money service as well.

Bridging divisions

The opposite of dividing a concept into parts is the bridging of parts to create one concept. As discussed earlier, polarization is just as much a commitment to a fixed way of looking at things as is a rigidly held concept. Polarization is simply a rigidly held two-concept situation. Instead of rigidly holding a spoon, one is rigidly holding a fork.

By putting together under a *single concept* things which have always been considered *apart*, one can open up new ways of looking at things. It may be that one thereby shifts attention away from the points of difference to the points of similarity. It may be that one realizes that the two separate concepts can be treated as manifestations of one overall concept. For instance, one could put together the concepts of "advertising" and "marketing" and look at them in terms of "availability" physically and mentally. Or one could put together the more divergent concepts of "production" and "marketing" to regard them both as movement/container situations. That is to say, flow through a container of varying size. The volume of flow matches up ultimately, but if the container is small the flow must be swift and must vary rapidly to match changing demands. On the other hand, in a large container the flow is slow at any point (though volume is large overall) and there is a certain reservoir function to smooth out changes in demand conditions. One can then go on to matching up different size containers and working out the advantages of each size or the proper mix.

Or one could consider the usual polarization between "responsibility" and "work". The basic idea is that some people have a decision responsibility for assessment, evaluation, and direction, and others are on the end of this decision and have to carry out the actual functions which are being directed. One could try bridging this gap and realize that evaluation, assessment, and changes could flow both ways. Also responsibility for accepting and innovating changes could flow upward as well as downward. Furthermore the worker is within some responsibility context toward his fellows, the union, his family, and the like. One could also realize that the "responsibility" function without some knowledge of the "work" function was pointless, since they were not separate but different parts of the same stream.

Even a simple polarization like "cause" and "effect" could be bridged over to give the idea of change chopped up at some conventional or convenient point, so that what comes before is called cause and what comes after is called effect. Thus one comes to realize that a cause is an ongoing process and does not only come about suddenly when a particular effect is manifest. This could apply to situations of labor unrest.

Like other lateral thinking procedures, bridging divisions is not a magic formula that has to produce results. It is part of an attitude that can change the way one looks at things and free one from fixed ideas. To begin with it may have to be used in a deliberate fashion, but after a while it easily becomes a habit. It is a habit which some people use anyway, but not many.

Judgment, evaluation, criticism, and the use of NO

7

This is the most fundamental section in the whole book. There are five reasons:

1. Because the place of judgment is the most crucial difference between lateral thinking and traditional vertical thinking.
2. Because the whole emphasis of education is directed toward critical evaluation.
3. Because unless one understands the different attitude toward judgment in lateral thinking, many of the procedures become impossible.
4. Because the different attitude toward judgment is the most difficult part of lateral thinking to accept since it is flatly contrary to traditional thinking habits.
5. Because the mind itself finds this aspect of lateral thinking unnatural.

Judgment, evaluation, criticism

Judgment, criticism, and evaluation are all aspects of the same thing. Judgment compares an idea with reality as defined by experience or compares one idea with another. Evaluation looks at an idea to see whether it is useful or whether it is worth exploring further. Criticism looks at an accepted idea to try to find faults in it.

The basic tool of all these processes is the word NO, the whole concept of the negative. The word itself may not be used but the basic function remains one of acceptance/rejection. NO is only a crystallization of this function. One may reject an idea because it is wrong or one may reject an idea because it is not as good as another idea (even though it is not wrong).

The process is that of finding one's way to usable ideas by rejecting others. It is a process of selection by exclusion. At every stage one excludes all that one can. Eventually one is left with an idea that cannot be excluded. That is the idea that one holds and uses.

In practice this rejection process is expressed in such ways as the following:
... that is not so
... that would not work
... that does not work
... that is not a valid conclusion
... that idea gets us nowhere
... that is not a new idea
... that would cost too much
... that is not practical
... that is irrelevant
... that shows a disregard for realities
... that shows a lack of experience in this field
... that is a stupid idea.

Vertical thinking and the rejection function

The rejection function is the very basis of vertical thinking. In vertical thinking, one proceeds from one state of information to another in a justified manner. If one had to explain the process of logic to someone who was unacquainted with it, one might well say that it consisted of being right at each step. Training in logical thinking involves making someone aware of increased opportunities to employ the rejected function. The difference between a good logical thinker and a poor one is that the former can say "no" more often. The other aspects of logic such as identification and transformation procedures all follow after the basic skill in handling the rejection function.

Education and the rejection function

● Education is soundly based on the need to be right all the time.
● The need to be right all the time is the biggest bar there is to new ideas.
● It is better to have enough ideas for some of them to be wrong than always to be right by having no ideas at all.
● The well-educated terror of being wrong breeds the arrogant certainty of being right.

In my own experience in the field of education, the one thing that has impressed itself on me has been the intense desire to have some means of judging at every moment whether a student's work is good or bad. Without such a means, educators feel unable to maintain their own direction, let alone impart a direction to their students. In practical terms it is difficult to quarrel with this point of view. But one can quarrel with the exclusive nature of an obsession with judgment wherever this is to be found. Training in vertical thinking is excellent—but it is not complete.

Lateral thinking and the rejection function

Because lateral thinking is not based on the rejection function, it becomes necessary to invent and use the term "lateral thinking". Without such a term confusion arises since one cannot *distinguish* between the type of thinking in which the rejection function is basic and the type in which it is not. Rather than ruin the effectiveness of vertical thinking by diluting the effectiveness of the rejection function, one preserves its absolute control in vertical thinking and differentiates this type of thinking from lateral thinking.

Practical use of the rejection function

Training can make a huge difference to the way the rejection function is used. Training in some fields markedly accentuates the use of the rejection function. Engineering is one such field. An engineer is trained to use the rejection function at as early a stage as he can. This is probably necessary in this field. Surrounded by a mass of possibilities the engineer can only proceed in a practical manner by throwing out as soon as possible any idea which can be rejected for any reason whatsoever. It may also be that in engineering mistakes simply cannot be tolerated. The difficulty of course is distinguishing between the design stage where mistakes may be essential for creativity, and the executive stage where mistakes are intolerable. Engineers themselves are the first to acknowledge this readiness to reject ideas. Another field is chemistry, but here the reason may be different. As a subject, chemistry is based on identification. Once one has identified a substance, one has unlocked the information regarding its behavior. Since identification is so crucial, the rejection function acquires a special importance.

Like chemistry, the management field tends to be an identification field. This may be based on experience, so that a manager has to decide from his own experience whether a new situation resembles an old one. It may also be that experience has thrown up certain unexplained but dogmatic rules, and in a confused situation the manager can only keep his feet by sticking to such rules with the use of a sharpened rejection function. Even in the case of more modern managers whose attitudes are based more on theory and measurement than on rules of thumb, the rejection function is relied on very heavily. Any manager is much more certain of the things he should not do than he is of the things he should be doing. This is very necessary, but it does make it difficult to understand a thinking process in which the rejection function is treated in a different way.

The different use of the rejection function

In lateral thinking an idea is protected from the rejection function. An idea which should have been rejected at once is allowed to survive. In fact, in lateral thinking an idea is no longer judged as to its correctness. This protection from the usual exercise of the rejection function is essential to lateral thinking. Once a new idea or a new approach has come about, then it can be judged in the usual way. But when the new idea has come about, lateral thinking has done its job and one switches into vertical thinking for evaluation.

Since the evaluation of an idea by vertical thinking nearly always follows the generation of the idea by lateral thinking, one could say that in lateral thinking judgment is delayed. In ordinary vertical thinking, judgment of an arrangement of information follows directly once this arrangement has come about. This is suggested in Figure 7-1. In lateral thinking judgment is delayed until the idea has had a chance to develop and also to set off other ideas. This delay may seem

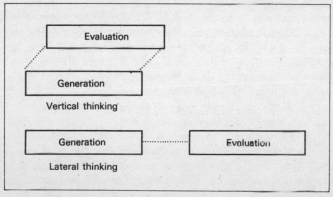

Figure 7-1.   81

a minor point since judgment is to be applied eventually, but it is vitally important because it allows an arrangement of information to have that stimulating effect which is so necessary for the restructuring of an idea.

Different use of information

In vertical thinking, an arrangement of information is used only for its correctness.

In lateral thinking an idea is used in order to bring about change. Vertical thinking is concerned with proof, lateral thinking with change. This means that a lateral thinker appreciates that an idea has a usefulness quite apart from its correctness.

A vertical thinker uses information in a backward manner. He is interested in describing what has happened. A lateral thinker uses information in a forward manner. He is interested in what happens *next*. A vertical thinker is concerned with catching up with what has happened in his mind. A lateral thinker is concerned with making something happen.

Right at each step

In vertical thinking, one has to be right at each step. So, no matter how many steps one takes, the end point (idea, solution, conclusion) is automatically right if all the intervening steps have been right. The process is illustrated diagrammatically in Figure 7–2. In this way one can move quite far from actual experience to reach distant and even

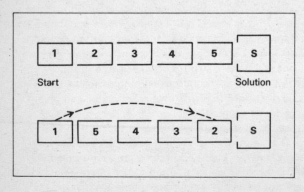

Figure 7–2.

unexpected conclusions. At the same time, one can be confident that these conclusions are valid—not because they seem right but because the process of reaching them has not included incorrect steps.

In lateral thinking one does not *have* to be right at each step, but one must be right at the *end*. Once one has reached a solution or a conclusion one cannot possibly justify it by the validity of the path by which it has been reached. One can try the new idea out to see if it works. One may be able to try the idea in practice, in a laboratory situation, or as a pilot project or test market. Nowadays one can try it out in a computer simulation. The increasing availability of computer simulations will make it more and more possible to judge ideas after they have come about, instead of depending for judgment on the way they have come about. Even without trial, the idea may be found to fit with reality so that a final judgment pronounces the idea sound. Or taking the new idea, one may be able to work backward to the starting position and show how a logical pathway could have been used to reach it. Once a sound logical pathway is constructed it cannot possibly matter whether it has come about before the new idea or after it.

In lateral thinking one does not *have* to make unjustified steps at each stage, but one is allowed to do so. At the end, the new idea may be reached by a line of logical development with only a single unjustified lateral jump along the way.

Intermediate Impossible

If one makes a logical step to a new idea, then that idea is automatically justified (at least in terms of the starting premises and concepts). But if one makes a lateral jump to a new idea, then that idea is not justified. There may be no way of telling whether it is right or wrong. Or the new idea may very clearly be wrong. Even if the new idea is obviously wrong, one still holds on to it and uses it as an "intermediate impossible". An intermediate impossible is an idea which one does not use for its own sake but as a stepping-stone to a new and useful idea.

The purpose of delaying the rejection function in lateral thinking is to allow one to use just such intermediate impossibles. Clearly, if one is allowed to use an intermediate impossible, then one is also allowed to use intermediate ideas which are not obviously wrong but simply *unproven*.

Reasons for protection

Why should one want to protect an idea from the rejection it deserves?

1. Because the idea may be rejected when judged within the old frame of reference, but if one holds on to the idea a new and more up-to-date frame of reference may come about and instead of being rejected the idea will make sense. (This phenomenon appears repeatedly in the world of art.)
2. Because even if the idea is nonsense at the moment and will always remain nonsense it can still trigger a useful idea. In a vertical thinking progression a useful idea could not arise from a useless one, but in lateral thinking it can easily do so.
3. Because one may have to pass through an intermediate impossible in order to reach a new idea.
4. Because an intermediate impossible may allow one to escape far enough from the old idea to be able to look at it objectively.
5. Because a new idea may not make sense at first, but if allowed to develop it will solidify and collect support until it does make sense in its own right.
6. Because by dropping (temporarily) the rejection attitude, one can start paying attention to the useful points of an idea instead of its weak points.

Dangers of the use of NO

Having considered some of the advantages to be gained by delaying the use of NO (the rejection function), one can consider some of the disadvantages that attend the too ready use of NO.

1. There is a great danger of being blocked by adequacy. As soon as one comes up with an idea which cannot be rejected, then one sticks with that idea. In fact, though this idea is adequate, there may be a whole lot of others which are far better, but which never get explored since NO cannot be used to proceed beyond the first adequate idea.
2. An arrogant righteousness attends any line of thought from which NO has been excluded. The validity of the path by which an idea has been reached imparts an absolute certainty to the idea. This can be very dangerous, for though the path may indeed be correct the conclusion can

never be more correct than the initial concepts with which one started. No logical processing, no matter how perfect, can justify an arbitrary set of starting premises.

3. One becomes very inhibited about putting forward ideas which cannot be absolutely justified before they are voiced. This means that the ideas used must all be compatible with the old framework. Hence the chances of being able to update this framework are very small. Also the possibility of an idea eliciting real support (information from others, et cetera) after it has been voiced is excluded.

4. A promising idea may be choked off because it does not have time to develop.

Practical effect of delaying judgment

The basic effect of delaying judgment is to allow an arrangement of information to exist in its own right and not only through reference to reality. This means that the idea can act as a focus for information from different sources, as a window through which to look at the old ideas, and as the seed of a new flowering of ideas. Basically the effect is a catalytic one. The unjudged idea does not take part in the final reaction but it may be necessary to bring that reaction about.

In this curbing of the rejection function one behaves as follows:

1. Does not rush to explore an idea to see why it will not work. (Does not try to show one's brilliance only through negative exercise of it.)

2. Does not reject an idea even if one knows it to be wrong from the outset.

3. Tries to prevent others from inhibiting ideas or rejecting them too soon. One may even reprieve ideas that have already been rejected and bring them back into consideration.

4. Does not at once set about trimming an idea to reduce it to a usable plan of action.

5. Can try to explain to others that if one is actually looking for new ideas there is a need to delay judgment.

The habit of delaying judgment can be applied:

1. To one's own internal thinking.

2. To the ideas one offers to others for their consideration.

3. To the ideas presented by others.

Of these three the second is by far the most difficult to achieve.

Thinking and action

It must be made quite clear that the delaying of judgment is meant to apply only to thinking and not to action. In fact, it applies only to one part of thinking—the generative stage of thinking, the first stage of thinking. Many people are hesitant about acquiring this habit because they feel that to attack the completeness of logical thinking is also to attack the necessity for logical action. This is not so at all. One could make out a case for provocative action in order to study patterns of response which could not otherwise be predicted or studied. But this would be a dangerous procedure because it would be impossible to foretell the full consequences of such action or even where it would be justified. It is better to confine the habit to the lateral stage of thinking.

The new functional word PO

When information is used in the usual way, it is subject to immediate judgment and possibly to rejection. When information is used in the lateral thinking way, judgment is delayed. If the setting is a formal one like a brainstorming session there is no difficulty in understanding how information is being used, but outside such a formal setting there could well be confusion. One of the functions of the new word PO is to indicate that the idea qualified by it is being used in a lateral thinking manner. This and other uses of the word PO are described later in Chapter 13.

Delayed judgment and lateral thinking techniques

Most of the lateral thinking procedures described so far have been straightforward, so straightforward in fact that they may appear quite logical. The techniques described in the following sections are much less straightforward and depend on the lateral use of information. This means the use of information not so much for its meaning but for the *effect* it has in setting off new ideas. This way of using information requires in every case the delaying of judgment, the withholding of the rejection function as described in this section.

If one were to consider the problem of a company which had to train special operators who then left to work for a company that had contributed nothing to their training, one could consider the problem in the way it was considered on page 70. Alternatively, one could make another outrageous lateral jump and see what ideas it set off. For instance, one might consider cutting off the legs of the operators so they could not leave. Such disadvantaged people could then be provided with amenities such as free transport to and from work. This would be possible for a corporation employing a large number of people but not for a small business. Thus the trained people would have a special reason for remaining with the large corporation which had trained them. One would move on to the idea of using cripples and then on to choosing to train healthy people who would nevertheless have some special reason for not moving. In the same way, one might pay attention to the advantages which a large corporation could offer, but which could not be offered by smaller businesses that might try to lure the operators away. Another outrageous idea would be to train people who were of limited intelligence. Much attention, however, would be paid to the training so that they would become skilled in performing a specific job with a high degree of skill. This skill would not, however, be transferable to a new job situation. Both these ideas are much less reasonable than the ones previously considered, yet they can still serve to set off new ideas. This is the type of procedure which is used in the techniques that follow.

Change and discontinuity

8

This section is as basic to lateral thinking as the section on the rejection function. One of the most important ways in which lateral thinking seeks to change ideas is through the introduction of discontinuity, through the use of the *discontinuity function*. The lateral thinking procedures described so far have all been based on current ideas. These current ideas have been identified, avoided, and changed around. The techniques to be described in the following sections involve the introduction of discontinuity.

What is discontinuity?

A discontinuity is a change which does not arise as part of the natural development of a situation. Thus, a sudden kink on a graph suggests that the basic situation has changed, that some new factor has come in. A discontinuity also implies that the new factor does not arise from within the situation but from outside. In its extreme sense, discontinuity implies that the new factor is not connected at all with the situation under consideration. For instance, if you were to look through a dictionary for a word which was relevant to the problem being discussed, that would show continuity. But if you were to use a table of random numbers to pick a word completely at random from the dictionary, then this word would introduce discontinuity since its choice was quite unconnected with the nature of the problem.

The word discontinuity is often applied when a connection cannot be seen. For example, a person watching chess for the first time may figure out the moves of all the pieces except the knight because the knight's move seems to be discontinuous. Indeed, the expression "knight's move" is often applied to the thinking of someone who moves from one idea to another, apparently unrelated, idea. In such cases the discontinuity is apparent, not real, for there is an underlying connection which is simply not visible to the observer. With true discontinuity, the person making the move from one idea to another does so without knowing of any connection. Nor is it a matter of a concealed connection which may be hidden from the person making the move. The situation is set up so that the move is truly discontinuous (like picking the word from a dictionary by means of a table of random numbers). This is a very pure form of discontinuity. Discontinuity, however, can also be useful when there is a reason concealed from the person making the move. That another person observing the jump can see a very valid reason for it cannot affect the discontinuity of the jump, which depends only on the person making it.

The purpose of discontinuity

Discontinuity can only be of use in a patterning system. In any other sort of system it would be pointless. Once the discontinuity has come about, it will cause a restructuring or a change of entry point.

It is the *effect* of the discontinuity on the current idea that matters, not so much the *nature* of the introduced factor. Although there is no reason for introducing the factor when it is introduced, a reason for doing so soon develops. Thus the reason comes after the event instead of before.

● There may not be a reason for saying something until after it has been said.

Normally, an idea develops until one is able to say something, perhaps to come to some conclusion. This conclusion arises directly from what has gone before. With lateral thinking, the idea can be introduced in a discontinuous fashion. Once it has been introduced, it alters the way the situation is being looked at and eventually a new way of looking at it develops. This new idea fully justifies the introduction of the discontinuity. The new idea may or may not actually incorporate the factor introduced; nevertheless, the effect of the discontinuity is justified by the usefulness of the outcome.

Once the discontinuous event has occurred, then a context slowly develops to support it. In a paradoxical way, being wrong and pig-headed can be useful because an unjustified position can gradually change the situation in order to justify that position. It was Bernard Shaw who remarked that progress was brought about by the unreasonable man, since the reasonable man adjusts to his environment whereas the unreasonable man tries to adjust his environment to himself.

Discontinuity and vertical thinking

Vertical thinking is essentially rational. That is to say, ideas hang together and make sense. One proceeds in an orderly sequence from one idea to another. In the section on the rejection function, it was pointed out that each step in the vertical thinking process has to be sound and justified. In the same way each step has to follow directly upon the preceding step. Unless this is so, one does not even get into a position to start judging whether the step is sound. So, in a sense, the continuity of the steps is even more basic than their soundness.

In lateral thinking one uses discontinuity quite deliberately and also makes use of it when it turns up by chance. In this regard (as with the use of the rejection function), lateral thinking flatly contradicts the rules of vertical thinking. That is why it is so necessary to have a clear idea of the distinctness of the two types of thinking, even though one may eventually need to use them both alternately and to switch from one to the other with ease.

As with the different use of the rejection function, the use of discontinuity in lateral thinking is a point of great difficulty for those whose training has been exclusively concerned with vertical thinking.

Link-up

No matter how truly disconnected an idea may be when it is introduced into the problem area, a connection will eventually develop. It is possible to take *any* problem and to take *any* word at random from a dictionary, and eventually a good connection between the two will develop. This happens because attention alternates from the problem to the random word until a context develops to include them both. As the full extension of the problem and of the random word are explored, a point is found where the two link up. This link-up provides a connection between the two. This connection gives a new entry point into the problem: an entry point which would not have developed from the nature of the problem (see Fig. 8–1).

Arranging discontinuity

If discontinuity involves the bringing in of something which has no connection at all with what is being considered, how can one organize this? If one goes through any selection

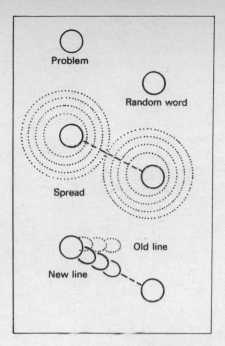

Figure 8–1.

process, one sees that selection is based on some frame of relevance and so the process is not really discontinuous. Should one not just sit around and wait for chance to provide discontinuity by bringing in what could not have been looked for? In fact there are some things one can do to introduce discontinuity:

1. Deliberately introduce discontinuity, by using, for example, a table of random numbers to pick a word from a dictionary.
2. Expose oneself to a variety of unsought-for and unprogrammed stimuli. The deliberate action is the exposure of entry into an environment rich with stimuli.
3. Quickly accept and appreciate things which do turn up by chance out of context.
4. Put together things which have no reason to be put together.

Relevance

Since any random word, object, or idea will eventually link in to the problem under discussion no matter how discontinuous its introduction, the terms "relevant" and "irrelevant" acquire a new meaning. Relevant means a thing which is relevant at the time of choice. Irrelevant means a thing that is chosen first and becomes relevant afterward. The important thing is that in becoming relevant it changes the context of the problem.

Figure 8–2 shows how a context of relevance surrounds the problem under discussion. A new item may fit into this context envelope. Another item introduced as a discontinuity does not fit in, but eventually the context changes itself to include the new item. And in so changing, the context allows new ideas and approaches which would have been excluded by the old context.

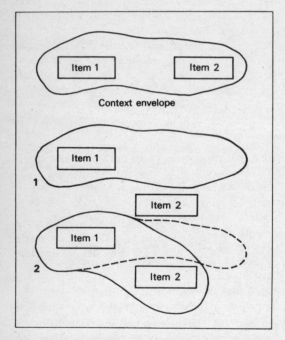

Figure 8–2.

The new word and the discontinuity function

One of the main uses of the new word PO is to introduce the discontinuity function. PO allows one to put together totally unconnected words and ideas in a way not ordinarily permitted. The purpose of such a discontinuous arrangement is to set off new ideas. This and the other functions of PO are described in detail in a subsequent section.

9

Group III: Change from within

The first group of lateral thinking procedures involved identifying the ideas that were dominating or tethering the way in which a situation could be looked at. For this first group, it was enough to *identify* the ideas. In the second group, efforts were made deliberately to *avoid* the current way of looking at a situation. In this third group, one takes the current way of looking at a situation and changes it around, then proceeds from that point.

In trying to generate new ideas, the most difficult thing is to get started. One may sit around for a long time if one waits for an idea to strike one. Even if one chooses not to wait, it is just as difficult to pluck an idea out of the air. What one requires is some *starting point*. Once one has a starting point, then one can watch it develop and look at the ideas that flow from it.

The easiest way to find a starting point is to take the current view of a situation or problem. Taken as it is, the current view is not much use as a starting point for developing new ideas since it will inevitably develop along conventional lines. So what one does is to take the current view and then change it round in a deliberate and unreasonable manner. The manner has to be unreasonable because if it were reasonable it would only be a conventional development of the idea.

Reversal

This means taking the current view and reversing it. By reversal is meant a whole group of changes which might be expressed as: turning it upside down; standing it on its head; turning it inside out; looking at it back to front; considering the direct opposite, et cetera. The point is that wherever a direction is implied it is quite easy to indicate the opposite direction (see Figure 9-1). This is why many people find this reversal procedure the easiest of all lateral thinking procedures.

It is usually possible to reverse a situation in a variety of different ways. Take, for instance, a car being driven down a road. This situation might be reversed in any of the following ways:

... the car is not being driven but is running away and taking the driver with it

... the car is riding in reverse down the road

... the car is moving along the road but in the opposite direction

... the car is not moving at all

... the car is standing still and the road is moving backward under the wheels.

There is no question of finding out which is the correct reversal. All of them are correct, for the purpose of reversal is to provide a means for changing a situation. There is no way of telling if the change is correct or not until it sets off useful new ideas. As with other lateral thinking procedures, change is what matters.

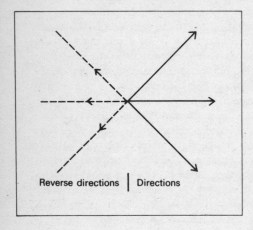

Reverse directions | Directions

Figure 9–1.

One could say that the chairman has called a board meeting. This would be reversed to "the board meeting has called the chairman". In fact this reversal immediately makes sense because it is the presence of ideas (or potential reactions) in the minds of the board members that actually caused the chairman to call a meeting. This leads to such ideas as whether the chairman is going to try to impose his ideas, judge the reaction to his ideas, or try to get advice from the board.

To ease traffic congestion in cities, one tries to discourage car parking by such things as meters. One could reverse this and try to encourage car parking by means of meters. This would mean that cars were allowed to park freely at meters. From this could come the idea of giving out-of-town shoppers a ticket for a specified day of the week, and display of the ticket on that day would allow free parking at any meter. This would spread the traffic load evenly over the week and also spread the load on stores. A side advantage might be that the use of meters by the shopping traffic might further discourage daily car commuters.

The purpose of advertising is to bring goods to the attention of the public. One could reverse this and say that the purpose of advertising is to remove goods from the public attention. This leads on to the idea that advertising does effectively remove the total product by concentrating attention on some particular feature of it. Perhaps one ought to rotate advertising through different features instead of concentrating on a supposed selling feature. Another reversal of the same starting theme might be that the purpose of advertising is to bring people to the attention of the goods. This would focus attention on how the goods reacted to the public. How adaptable were the products to test market reactions? Could the product be changed depending on the behavior of the public or is it the behavior of the public which ought to be changed?

Productivity in service industries rises at a much lower rate than in manufacturing industries. In some areas such as health or education, productivity seems to be going in reverse insofar as the increasing quality of service requires more manpower and equipment. One of the main problems is to find some way of measuring the productivity of a service industry, since there is no fixed output which can be valued. One could make a simple reversal and measure not the productivity of the service but the "negative productivity" of doing without it. What would be the cost of doing without the service? This approach might be difficult where the costs are usually long term and thus difficult to estimate (for example, education) or where human values are involved (for example, health). A different reversal would involve measuring not the increase in productivity but the decrease in productivity. This would mean that at any stage a real increase in costs would be noted. Then a percentage decrease in those costs would be regarded as a percentage increase in productivity, as shown in Figure 9–2.

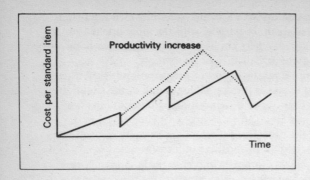

Figure 9–2.

Some general points can be made about using the reversal procedure:

- Do not worry about whether your change is a true reversal or not.
- Once you have made a reversal, stay with it for a while even though no immediate ideas are set off. Give it time to develop.
- No reversal can be too outrageous. No reversal should be passed over as being too impossible.
- In considering the reversal and the initial ideas that spring from it, you need to delay judgment as described in the preceding section.
- The reversal is only a starting point, not a solution. Your ideas may stray so far that they eventually have little to do with the starting point.

Distortion and exaggeration

This procedure is similar to the reversal procedure in that one takes the current view and alters it in an unreasonable manner in order to set off new ideas. In this case the change is not one of reversal but of distortion or exaggeration. This may mean taking part of the current situation and changing it around, or it may mean carrying a process to an extreme conclusion. For instance, one may be considering how much time research workers should be allowed to work on their own ideas. One could then go on to say that they should spend all their time working on their own ideas at the company's expense. From this would arise the idea of selling their research efforts, as from a research institute. One could then move on to the notion of buying research from a research establishment instead of running one's own. One might even end up with a twin system in which a research institute was set up in parallel with the more applied research, and researchers could rotate through them both according to time, demand, or inclination.

The point about distortion or exaggeration is that when it is sufficient it makes it impossible to look at the situation in the original way or to develop it along conventional lines. Once one has been forced to make a switch to a new approach, the development may then be quite conventional.

Overcapacity in the fertilizer industry resulted from highly optimistic market forecasts and changes in ammonia technology which increased productivity. One could take this situation and distort it to the point where production was so cheap that fertilizer could be given away. From this impossible idea, one could move on to the idea of expanding the market by actually giving it away to areas which were not part of the established market. One might in fact have some sort of agreement whereby fertilizer would become part of the aid to underdeveloped countries. One might even extend the distortion to suggest that the market was completely saturated, and that fertilizer companies should diversify into irrigation and desalination projects to create new markets.

Distortion and exaggeration are often the first step in a design project. The simplest form of originality in art consists in distorting reality to the point where the grotesque and the bizarre become forms in their own right. If you ask people (including engineering students) to redesign the human head, the results show a uniform distortion or exaggeration of what is already there. For instance, there will be a number of designs with eyes at the back of the head and a number with four eyes—one at each corner. Another change is that the neck will be made longer and more flexible or the ear flaps removed.

A problem of quality control might arise in the manufacture of a product. One could tackle this in a number of ways. One might increase the number of inspectors or use more frequent sampling. One might give incentives for fault-free assembly if it was that sort of product. Or one might do nothing about it but set up a very efficient replacement service to deal with complaints. Another approach would be to exaggerate the situation until every single product was faulty so that no faults could be noticed. From this would come the idea of redesigning the product rather than trying to spot or eliminate faults.

The problem might be one of trimming excessive office expenses. One might exaggerate this situation to one where people were all paid to sit around and do nothing. From this would arise the idea of actually paying someone to sit around and do nothing except keep her eyes open for ways to cut expenses. This would be a job in itself, and it would last so long as it was productive in turning up ways of reorganizing or saving money. Another idea arising from the original exaggeration would be to pay people to sit around for a day or two to discuss reorganization instead of letting it drift on. Or again one might pay an outside consultant precisely to do nothing. That is to say, one would pay him in the hope that his lack of recommendations would show that the expenses were not excessive and that cost-saving efforts would be better applied elsewhere.

There are some general points in using the distortion/exaggeration change:

● Make only one distortion or exaggeration at a time. Otherwise confusion will result.

● The distortion or exaggeration does not have to be very extreme to be effective.

● As well as seeing what ideas the change sets off, try to follow the direct effects of the distortion or exaggeration on the situation.

● As with reversal, once you have made the change stay with it for a while instead of trying change after change until one seems fertile.

Change from outside. 10
Group IV:
Discontinuity
methods

Exposure

If you set out to look for something you will probably find
it. In any case you will know what you are looking for. The
clearer you are about what you are looking for the easier
your search will be, since you can tell at once what is
irrelevant. The trouble with knowing what you are looking
for is that you have little chance of coming up with something other than what you are looking for. The more
knowledge one has, the more restricted is one's field of
search because there is less that satisfies the detailed requirements. This is suggested in Figure 10–1. Yet there are some
very useful ideas which one would never look for but once
found prove valuable. These are ideas which one would only
set out to look for *after they have been found*.

In the exposure method one does not simply relax the
rules of relevance, one deliberately sets out to consider things
that are irrelevant. Since you cannot choose something that
is "irrelevant", you can only expose yourself to irrelevant
influences. What you do is to put yourself in a setting which
is rich in irrelevant influences. These influences are not
irrelevant in themselves but only to your problem, your ideas,
or your field of study. In effect you are exposing yourself to
the happy accidents of chance. Coupled with this exposure is
a readiness to follow up ideas that are suggested by chance.

Such exposure may take the form of wandering around a
toy shop or a chain store, or going to an exhibition that has
nothing to do with your problem. For instance an accountant
might find himself wandering around an exhibition of wig-
making equipment. Exposure may involve visiting different
countries. Exposure may involve opening a journal at random
and reading whatever feature was to be found at that page.
● The point about exposure is that it must be deliberate,
  otherwise the necessary attitude of mind is lacking.

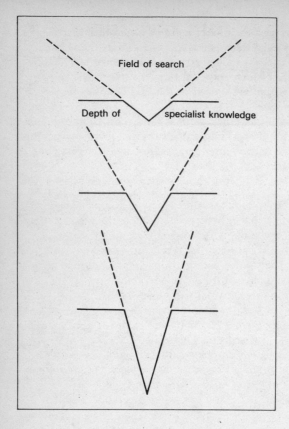

Field of search

Depth of specialist knowledge

Figure 10–1.

● The nature of the exposure does not matter so much as
its irrelevance.

In using the exposure method, one may just wander about
until something catches one's fancy. For some people this
may be successful. For others who are not especially familiar
with the procedure it is best to pick out something to be
attended to. This selection is entirely capricious. It may involve picking up a plastic duck in a toy-shop when one has
management organization problems. Having selected the
area of attention, one stays with it and tries to see how it
could relate to the problem in hand. For instance, the duck
might suggest two layers of organization: the above-surface
organization and the true, hidden (below-surface) organization channels. The above-surface organization is concerned
with the official status hierarchy, but the below-surface
organization depends on cross-hierarchy channels between

people who trust each other and find each other effective. Should one align these two layers or facilitate the natural development of the hidden structure? One may pick up an object in this fashion and even buy it to take home and put on one's desk so that it stays in the field of consciousness as a discontinuity.

● In using the exposure method there must be a readiness to reach out and find significances and relationships. But this must happen *after* an attention area has arisen and not before.

● New ideas or lines of thought may be triggered off at the time of exposure. Even if no such ideas arise immediately, the influences will be stored away and can come up later quite unexpectedly.

The main problem with the exposure method is where to draw the line. The field of relevant material is large enough. By definition the field of irrelevant material is infinite. One could easily spend all one's time looking only at irrelevant material and coming up with the odd good idea now and then. After all there are 60,000 technical periodicals published each year. The amount of time spent in exposure to random influences is a matter of judgment and balance. There are two different situations to be accounted for:

1. If you have run out of ideas either in innovation, design, or problem solving, then it is worth spending deliberate time in exposure until you get going again.

2. As a matter of routine, it is worth making a habit of exposure to random influences. This might be a very small amount of time, perhaps two hours a month visiting an unrelated exhibition or reading one unrelated feature (not a general magazine feature) in a journal once a week.

The actual time spent in deliberate exposure to random influences is not important. Nor is the nature of the material. Nor are the ideas that arise on such occasions. What is important is the attitude of mind that follows from using this procedure: an attitude that makes one sensitive to ideas and influences that turn up without being looked for. Such sensitivity has always been the basis of progress in science and innovation in business.

Cross-fertilization

This is really very similar to the exposure method except that the random environment is provided by *people*, not by things.

- Cross-fertilization may mean listening to people in other fields talking about their own subject.
- Cross-fertilization may mean bringing together a group of people from different fields to talk about your problem.
- Cross-fertilization may mean tackling a problem in a field different from your own.

The important point about cross-fertilization is that the people should *really* be from very different fields. It is not so much a matter of using a generalist who can work in system terms within any field. It is a matter of using someone who has definite expertise acquired in one field and a definite point of view that arises from that field. Such a person may not be able to contribute directly to your problem, but out of his approach to your problem you, yourself, may be able to develop a new idea.

As in the exposure procedure, the main point is that the other person should be irrelevant. It is the view from outside that matters, not the fact that under the surface most disciplines are pretty similar anyway.

As a matter of course it is probably better to use experts in their own field rather than dabblers. This is not to say that a dabbler cannot come up with extremely good ideas, or that someone who is in no sense an expert cannot provide the right answer to a problem. It is more a matter of using the expert as a *window* so that you can see right into his field and then generate your own ideas. One can divide these two approaches:

1. Ideas directly supplied by outsiders who may have no special knowledge.
2. Transfer of ideas or processes from one field to another.

Cross-fertilization may occur casually in conversation, in deliberately assembled group meetings, through suggestion-slip schemes, by listening to other people talking about their own fields. The important point to be clear about is that you may be asking an outsider how he would tackle your problem, but apart from this you want to see how he tackles his problems.

Cross-fertilization does have a great drawback which is largely absent from the exposure method. The drawback is that people do talk a lot. It is possible to waste a great deal of time discussing everything with committees and groups. Any cross-fertilization system set up deliberately often grows until it takes up more time than it is worth. Once one is aware of this danger, it is possible to keep it in check. Talk tends to have a self-generating effect. The point of cross-fertilization is not so much discussion or debate but a sparking of new ideas.

Problem switching

In a way this procedure is a mixture of cross-fertilization and exposure. Like these other procedures, it is an attempt to bring in something from outside a particular problem area and through such discontinuity to set off new ideas. Problem switching simply consists of changing from one problem to another before the first problem has been completed. This may take several forms.

1. When a person has been tackling a particular problem for a long period of time he can be switched over to another problem. This can be done by re-allocating problems in a research department, but this is not as satisfactory as changing to a new setting.

2. A person may keep two problems going in parallel and switch from one to another as he feels inclined or according to some fixed time scale. This may happen naturally when a person has some absorbing hobby which becomes his alternative problem source in the home situation.

3. In a problem-solving situation one may deliberately set up two problems and then switch back and forth between them, spending about one hour on each in rotation.

If one does set up a deliberate problem-switching situation, then the two problems ought to be as different as possible. For instance, one problem may be of an organizational nature and the other of a physical nature. It does not really matter whether the people involved are capable of solving the physical problem so long as it provides a different kind of mental effort. An operations research team, for instance, could switch from a retail distribution problem to designing a new toothbrush.

Though it can be very fruitful, problem switching is rather difficult to implement in a research department. A person who is taken off one problem is apt to feel that he has failed. He resents it even more if another person working alongside him is put onto the problem. When people are working on problems, they tend to get very possessive and subjective about them. In this situation, it is better to allow the problem to be in abeyance while the man works on a new (short-term) problem, and then let him go back to the original problem; or combine the two by asking him to tackle the short-term problem in parallel with the other one.

An essential point in problem switching is that the person can return at once to the old problem if some new ideas are sparked by the alternative problem. The original problem is being held in limbo while the alternative one is tackled, but there is complete access to that limbo. This possibility is unfortunately excluded if a research worker is shifted to a new department or has his problem turned over to someone else.

Some people appear to flit from one problem to another without ever solving any of them. This "butterfly" mind approach irritates practical people who wish to see things tackled one at a time and in order. The two are not in conflict. Problem switching is only used when there is no progress otherwise. Nor is problem switching an open-ended flight to another and yet another problem. It is quite true that in the end the butterfly minds (if properly motivated) do come back and solve all the problems, but in a practical situation one may not be able to wait that long. For practical purposes problem switching can be a formal, contained situation and yet be effective. As usual one has to steer between the polarization of those who feel that any freedom leads to impractical chaos and those who feel that any structure inhibits originality.

Change from outside. 11
Group V: Deliberate
introduction of
discontinuity

The preceding discontinuity procedures have all involved
some sort of exposure to irrelevant influences as a means of
introducing discontinuity. The procedures described in this
section involve the deliberate introduction of discontinuity.
These deliberate introduction methods are more practical in
the sense that they take up much less time. After all, in
exposure methods one has to *wait* for something to happen.
On the other hand, the exposure methods are much better
for developing the exploratory attitude of mind.

Analogies

A number of effective methods for generating new ideas are
based on the use of analogies. As has been mentioned before,
one of the major difficulties in generating new ideas is to get
going. The advantage of an analogy is that it has a life of its
own. For instance, in the analogy of going fishing the process
is so well known that one moves from one step to another
without difficulty: finding time, choosing a stretch of water,
perhaps getting a license, preparing the rod and tackle,
choosing a position by the water, selecting bait, changing
bait, moving about, patience, catching something, or the fish
that got away, fishermen's stories, and so on.

In using the analogy method, one translates the problem
situation into an analogy and then develops the analogy in
its own right. From time to time, one translates back to the
real problem to see what would happen if the process taking
place in the analogy took place in the problem situation. For
instance, the fishing analogy might have been used in considering a management recruitment problem. "Stretch of
water" would now read area of exploration, perhaps campus,
perhaps business college, perhaps other corporations. "Bait"
would now read salary, fringe benefits, stock options, promotion prospects, status, responsibility, location, or others.

"Fishing tackle" would now read advertising media, personal contact, interviews, word of mouth, and the like. One would then come to the point when no fish were being caught. What could be responsible for this? Perhaps those waters were overfished, perhaps the bait was unsuitable, perhaps the weather conditions were not right, perhaps it was a matter of too little patience. One might then consider whether the object of the fishing was sport, the odd chance of getting something really worthwhile, or the need to have some fish to eat. If it was the last, one might consider buying fish from a professional fish catcher, buying frozen fish from a store and spending extra time cooking it, or even changing the menu so that frozen fish fitted in (fresh salmon might dominate a menu but fish fingers would not). Translated back into the problem situation, this would all mean that if changing the incentives and the search area were unsuccessful, then one ought to have more patience, or employ professional search agencies, or decide to spend more time on executive training on the job, or even tailor the job in such a way that exceptional executive talent was no longer required.

In mathematics, one translates a situation into the symbols of a formula and then lets the formula run along its own course of development. At the end, one translates back. This is the way one uses analogies except that one does not only translate back at the end but all the way along as well.

Analogies serve as vehicles for processes, functions, relationships, and it is these which are being transferred to the original problem and tried out to see if they fit or what ideas they set off. The natural development of an analogy is quite unrelated to the actual problem and so it provides a source of discontinuity. The problem is forced (or encouraged) to develop along a line different from its natural development.

The use of an analogy to get a problem moving is quite a different thing from arguing by analogy. No matter how good the fit, the development of an analogy can *prove* nothing about the development of the problem situation. As usual in lateral thinking, the way one arrives at a new idea can never by itself justify that idea. The idea must stand in its own right.

How does one choose an analogy? There is a danger that if the analogy is too natural and too good a fit, then its development will simply carry the problem along a path it might have followed anyway. On the other hand, if the analogy is too outrageous it might be so difficult to translate it back into the terms of the problem that no development at all occurs. The fishing analogy chosen earlier was probably too close an analogy, so the ideas turned up by its use were rather routine. Other analogies might have been buying a new suit, looking for antiques, stamp collecting, frying an egg. All these analogies except the last one involve a search procedure for something that has to fit into some specific setting. Though very different in nature, the egg-frying analogy could set off ideas about job appeal (different taste in fried eggs, sunny-side up, et cetera), about timing, about sticking to the present job (sticking to the pan), and transfer devices (egg slices).

● The most important thing about the choice of an analogy is that it should be vivid and have a *definite life* of its own.
● The second most important thing about the choice of an analogy is that it should be full of concrete images and happenings. A concrete analogy is usually much more fertile than an abstract one.
● The third most important thing about an analogy is that something must be *happening*. There must be a process of change. Mere description of a scene is not much use.
● An analogy should be a well-known process rather than a description of a specific occasion.

Certain suppliers of heavy industrial equipment with a limited market have the recurring problem that demand may be intermittent and enormous when it occurs. This sort of situation occurs with suppliers of generating equipment to electricity generating boards. Instead of a constant trickle of demand, there are huge lumps at intervals. To some extent this is inevitable, for advancing technology and costs make it desirable to change over suddenly to completely new methods, and to require that all the equipment be uniform and up to the latest technological developments. The result is either very slow delivery, or tremendous overcapacity if the supplier tries to meet the size of the sudden demand. For this problem, one might use as an analogy a visit to the dentist with toothache. One might know that toothache is likely to occur at some time but one does not know exactly when (breakdown in equipment). But when it does occur, one requires full-scale attention immediately. One expects that the dentist should have this full-scale capacity always available. If such capacity is not immediately available, one must look around to find another dentist who can supply the demand.

An important feature is that the sudden need for dental treatment cannot be met by a continued supply of a small amount of attention. The attention must meet the demand when it happens—and meet it fully. Another feature is that dental treatment is tailored to a particular customer, to meet his particular requirements.

All these features can be translated without too much difficulty to the supply, for instance, of heavy electricity generating equipment. Or, rather, the breakdown in electricity supplies could be regarded as the breakdown in the health of the teeth, and the supply of generating equipment as the dental treatment. In the case of teeth, one might take X-rays at intervals to keep an eye on what was happening. This would correspond to regular surveys of demand for electricity and the state of generating equipment. From the idea of false teeth would come the suggestion that there should be a shift to interchangeable units which were not specifically tailored to one customer but could be adapted to that customer's needs. On the other hand, such units could be marketed on a wider basis and there would be less dependence on the fluctuating demand of a single customer. In dentistry, the borderline between repair and replacement is small. Perhaps one could design units which did not have to be totally replaced but could be replaced bit by bit. Paying the dentist a sudden large sum at an unexpected time might not be very satisfactory to dentist or patient. Perhaps it would be better to pay a regular retaining fee in anticipation of service. Perhaps some method of continued financing might make life easier for the suppliers of intermittent demand equipment. Perhaps the suppliers should become part of the service they are supplying.

● The problem situation suggests a type of analogy, and then the development of that analogy suggests a development of the problem which may be different from its own natural development. In this way new ideas can emerge.

Random word

The use of random word stimulation is the most definite of the methods for introducing discontinuity. It is also the most deliberate. Paradoxically, even though it is the most deliberate it also introduces the purest form of discontinuity.

In the exposure methods, one deliberately puts oneself into a situation where one might be influenced by unsought-for stimuli. Nevertheless, one has chosen the situation and to some extent one chooses to pay attention to a particular stimulus. The same thing applies to cross-fertilization, problem switching, and even the analogy method. In most of these methods, one has to wait for the random influence to appear. In the random word method, one very deliberately generates a random stimulus. And the way one generates it is truly random. Thus this particular method is in a sense a summary of all the other methods and the most extreme form of discontinuity.

The characteristics of the random word method are the characteristics of all the discontinuity methods, and they can be listed as follows:

1. The stimulus comes from outside.
2. The stimulus is truly irrelevant (not chosen in any way).
3. By being brought into the problem situation, discontinuity is introduced.
4. The stimulus links up with the problem situation and establishes a new entry point or approach.
5. The stimulus becomes relevant *after* it has brought about its effect.

The fundamental point of discontinuity is that the choice of material is not dictated by relevance. But that relevance becomes established *after* the material has been chosen.

The most convenient source of random words is a dictionary, but one could use a specially prepared list of random words for use on any problem (about 100 words). This would not work if it were prepared for a specific problem, because the words would tend to have relevance to the problem. One can also use any written material whatever and simply select a word by randomly specifying a line number and word position along that line.

The purest random procedure would be to use a table of random numbers to select a page in the dictionary (for example, 2, 3, 8 would select page 238), and then get some more numbers to select the word position on that page (for example, 1, 4, 6 would select word position 14, counting down the page unless there were 146 or more words on that page). A simpler way is to pick a page number by just thinking of a number and then a word position in the same way. This is not truly random since one knows that the earlier pages deal with the earlier letters of the alphabet, but it is random enough since no one would remember all the word positions.

It may happen that the word selected in this way is a preposition or a conjunction. If so, one simply moves on to the next word. Nouns are easier to use than verbs, adjectives, or adverbs, so one moves down the page from the selected position until one comes to the first noun. Then one stays with that word as the random stimulus.

The first noun may seem very unpromising. Nevertheless, one must stay with it. It is quite useless to move on until one comes across a word which seems promising. This would be selection according to preconceived ideas, and so the whole point of using a random word to introduce discontinuity would be lost. Nor is it any good closing the dictionary and trying again. This is a very important point, because as soon as any element of preference creeps in, the whole purpose of a random word is lost. Moreover the effort to use a random word is much reduced if one is inclined to move on to another easier one. For this reason it is best not to use more than one random word at any session. This way, one learns to make use of the first word. Otherwise, one may make only a feeble effort and then say, "That one doesn't seem much good, let's move on to another one." Often it is from the apparently unpromising words that the best ideas arise. It is certainly difficult at first, but gradually one develops confidence and skill in the method.

Once found, the random word is held in the same attention envelope as the problem situation. After a while, some sort of link-up will develop between the two. The link-up may be direct or indirect. For instance, there may be a pun on the random word. Or the random word may suggest a song and something in that song is relevant to the problem. Or the random word may lead on to another word which can link up with the problem.

In order to generate the link-up, one pays attention to the random word and develops it in all possible directions. At each point, one refers back to the problem to see what relevance this new development could have.

For instance, the problem might be one of devising incentives for a sales force. The random word selected was *gong*. This could be developed in the following ways:

Gong—used for announcements: Publish lists of top performing salesmen.

Gong—slang term for a medal or decoration: Give awards

or privileges which would have more than a monetary value (access to a special club, for example).

Gong—a noise that is loud but brief: Instead of giving permanent incentives give short-burst incentives; very high value commission incentives but sustained only over a short period (to give the salesmen confidence in what they could do).

In using random words, one can stick to a particular line of development, but it is best to develop as many lines as possible at first. Later on one can follow through in depth any of the original approaches.

How long should one spend trying to make sense of a random word? There is no special time limit, but there is a danger of boredom and frustration if one spends too long. With skill and experience, one can make full use of a random word in as little as three minutes. That is enough to relate any conceivable problem to any random word. To begin with, five minutes might be more suitable. Within that five minutes, one develops the random word in as many ways as possible, and through this development links it in to the problem. If nothing at all seems to be happening, then one can spend as long as ten minutes in waiting and trying. But beyond that it gets tedious. After the ten minutes have passed, it is better not to try another word but to use another method. A new random word can be tried on a new occasion. There is not much point in keeping the random word in mind all day as one tries to effect a link-up. In using random words, the emphasis is on using them in a hurry, in trying to generate and note down all the ideas as quickly as possible.

There is no question of there being any one right way to use a particular random word. Any and every way is right, so long as something is happening. Within a group of people, there will be several completely different uses made of the same random word in the same problem setting.

The random word technique can be used in a group setting and it is often more fertile under these circumstances. But the main advantage of the technique is that it can be used quite deliberately by one person on his own and at any time he wishes. If one makes a habit of spending just three minutes a day applying this technique to any current problem, the payoff can be considerable. It is best not to go on beyond three minutes even when the ideas are flowing. To limit the procedure to three minutes is much more useful than to generate some extra ideas but make the procedure unusable because the time is not defined.

The main thing with the random word technique is the acquiring of confidence. At first it seems incredible that a truly random word can have any use at all. The procedure is totally opposite to traditional, analytical procedures which seek only the relevant and vital. But when one realizes that the way the mind works makes it impossible for any stimulus to remain irrelevant once it has been brought into the same attention area as something else, then one starts to acquire confidence.

Random word stimulation depends on the patterning nature of mind for its effect. The random word can open up a new entry point, and a change of entry point is one of the most powerful ways of changing the way a problem is approached. A new entry point can mean that the old pattern comes to be used in a new way and can lead to a new conclusion.

As usual with lateral thinking, the random-word technique is not a method for finding solutions but a method for generating new ideas. Solutions may arise directly from the new ideas or only after considerable processing by vertical thinking. Change is what one is looking for.

In 1970, investment in containerized cargo services at European ports was well ahead of the use of these facilities. Each port vied with its rivals to provide container cranes and handling equipment. Most of this remained idle. The problem is one of how far to invest in a developing trend. Clearly, the ports with container facilities might expect to attract the container traffic ahead of their rivals. To hang back would be fatal. And yet the sheer efficiency of container operations would mean an overall diminution in the port facilities required. Hence, much of the investment would remain unused, at least for a long time. The problem is a general one which arises when a facility has to be developed ahead of a demand.

A random word picked out of a dictionary was *oath*. How can this be related to the problem?

Oath—used to imply certainty: How much certainty could there be about the forecast development of container traffic— certainty perhaps that it would happen but not when or where—planning within an envelope of certainty but without the details.

Oath—implying promises and permanence: Need one invest to show the permanent availability of handling facilities? Would it not be enough to show the availability to meet any growing demand—keeping slightly ahead of demand—leasing of equipment rather than purchase, perhaps setting up a permanent leasing pool financed by the rival ports with the ability to switch equipment on demand.

Oath—legally binding according to the rules of the game: Is it correct to assume that containerized cargo handling will follow the procedures of precontainer handling? Perhaps there has been failure to realize the different nature of the operation.

Oath—a ritual declaration: A ritual gesture by port authorities to maintain the present status of their ports; development by continuity rather than forward planning even though it gives that appearance.

Oath—a one-sided form of communication, a reaction (as in swearing at someone): Would it not be better to co-operate with container shipping groups for joint investment in handling facilities, or even joint investment in the shipping side?

Suppose the problem is the pricing of a new cosmetic item such as water-soluble quick-tan gels. Let the random word be *instinct*.

Instinct—don't try to reason it out but ask trade salesmen whose experience in such matters has become a reliable instinct.

Instinct—fixed patterns of buying: Into which fixed pattern can this item be slipped (for instance, holiday buying, routine buying, luxury buying)? How far can the price be stretched without disrupting the pattern?

Instinct—fear, avoidance: Is the item one where the quality difference might be just enough to persuade people to avoid a cheaper item and so allow a large price increase in the better quality item? Can the item become an obligatory buy or can its purchase be avoided?

Instinct—inherited expectation: Does the item have to fit into the expected price range of established products, or can it be established on its own outside this expectancy?

Both these examples show how an apparently unrelated word can be related to a problem in a way which makes sense. In neither case were any of the ideas extreme or un-realistic. If, however, one had exhausted all the more reasonable approaches, then one might deliberately encourage more outrageous suggestions.

The random word method has several advantages:

● It takes little time.
● It can be carried out on one's own.

- It is a deliberate process (as distinct from waiting for an effect).
- It should produce some result.

In using the random word method, the important thing to remember is that it requires confidence and experience before it becomes fully effective. The first time a random word is used it may seem awkward and unprofitable. But it gets easier each time.

Lateral thinking is a way of using information to escape from
old ideas and generate new ones. This special way of using
information involves an attitude of mind, the use of various
techniques, and the use of a new functional word. In addition, there are formal settings which encourage the use of
lateral thinking. These formal settings could be regarded as
techniques or as envelopes within which various lateral
thinking methods can be used.

Most of these formal settings are for use by groups as
distinct from individuals. Such settings are no substitute for
individual skill in lateral thinking. On the other hand, the
settings are valuable because they do provide a definite
structure for the encouragement of the lateral thinking
process. There is some danger, however, that the formal
settings come to be regarded as the process itself instead of
simply an *opportunity* for its use. For instance, it is a mistake
to assume that lateral thinking is the same thing as a brainstorming session. What goes on in such a session is very
largely lateral thinking, but the session is only one expression
of certain aspects of lateral thinking. The convenience of such
sessions is an advantage, but the notion that lateral thinking
can be used only in such sessions is a disadvantage.

Brainstorming
The brainstorming session was originated by Alex Osborne
and has since become a much used setting for stimulating
creative thinking. The brainstorming session is described here
not so much as a creative tool but as a setting for the
practice of lateral thinking. The main features of brainstorming may be summarized as follows:
1. Formality of the setting.
2. Separation of evaluation from generation of ideas.
3. Interaction and stimulation of ideas.

Formality
The paradox is that one of the most useful features of the

brainstorming session is its formality. This may seem strange when the purpose of a session is to encourage the informal flow of ideas. Yet it is because of the formality of the structure that, within it, informal methods of using information can flourish. The lateral use of information is so different from the ordinary use of information as encouraged by education and training that most people find it useful to have a special session. It is rather like having a fancy-dress ball where one is not embarrassed to dress up because everyone else is dressed up as well, and after all that is the purpose of the ball. When one enters a brainstorming session, one can put on a special "imaginary" cap which frees one to think in a different way. When one leaves the session one takes the cap off. A brainstorming session provides a specific holiday from the rigid logic of everyday management. The formality of a brainstorming session consists of the special name of the session, a defined purpose, and a limited time. The formal structure within the session is much less important than the formal envelope within which the session takes place.

Generation and evaluation of ideas

The separation of the evaluation of ideas from their generation is common to all creative thinking methods. Such a separation is fundamental to lateral thinking and is considered in section 7 on page 81. A brainstorming session carries this separation to its logical conclusion by making the purpose of the session a generation of ideas and leaving evaluation to a subsequent follow-up session. Evaluation of ideas is forbidden in a brainstorming session. Such a complete ban is much easier to work with than a simple delay in evaluation of an idea after it has come about.

Once the participants in a brainstorming session know that their task is generation of ideas, not judgment, they become able to think more laterally. This is especially so if they know that evaluation will be carried out in a subsequent session. This knowledge relieves them of the responsibility of suggesting flawed ideas. Even so, the most difficult aspect of a brainstorming session is to prevent evaluation.

Evaluation occurs when one member of the group can immediately see why an idea would not work or why it would be impractical because of cost. The natural tendency is to criticize the idea. This is very marked when one member

116

of the group happens to have special knowledge so that it is much more obvious to him than to the others that the idea is unworkable. He then feels a compulsion to share his special knowledge with the others.

Certain types of training (for example, engineering, accountancy) so encourage immediate evaluation of ideas that people with these trainings find brainstorming sessions very frustrating, at least in the beginning.

The urge to comment on the practicality of the ideas of others is matched by the habit of criticizing one's own ideas before they are offered to others. This is in fact a much bigger danger. Criticism of the ideas put forward by others can be stopped by a good chairman. But if a participant mentally rejects an idea before he even presents it, no one else can benefit from that idea. One of the main reasons for being very firm with those who do criticize the ideas of others is that they make people very self-critical. A person who has managed to resist evaluating an idea himself resents having it evaluated in an obvious manner by someone else.

Evaluation of an idea can take several forms:
1. Whether the idea would work at all.
2. Whether it would be practical.
3. Whether the cost of implementing it would be too high.
4. Whether the idea is new.

The last type of evaluation is not directed at the worth of the idea but at whether it is novel. The purpose of a brainstorming session is indeed to generate new ideas rather than to list old ones. Nevertheless, an idea which has just occurred to someone as a new idea should be treated as such even though others taking part in the session might be able to say: "That's not new"; "We've thought of that already"; "We've tried that some time ago". Unless a person is directly involved in a field, it is quite likely that he will come up with ideas that have been thought of. Yet a brainstorming session should include people who are not directly involved in the field. If such people were to be made cautious about putting forward ideas because they might not be new enough, then the spontaneity of the session would be ruined.

It is very much easier to forbid evaluation of any sort rather than to try to define which sort of evaluation is permissible.

Random stimulation and interaction of ideas

Brainstorming is a group activity. The advantage of the group is that ideas offered by one person can spark different ideas in another person. Different people have different ways of looking at things. Different people put information together in different ways. One person may initiate an idea and develop it in one way, while another person develops it in quite a different way. In a brainstorming session on the use of railway lines, one person suggested that they might be used as guidelines for free-flying air vehicles. Another person took up the idea of guidelines and suggested that the rights-of-way acquired for railway lines could be used for routing pipelines and cables.

One person may come to a dead end with an idea that another person can pick up and develop with great imagination.

In a brainstorming session, the stimulation is not as truly random as it is in deliberate random stimulation (for instance, by taking a word from a dictionary), for the ideas have all arisen in connection with the problem being considered. Nevertheless, the ideas do come from "outside" one's own way of looking at the problem. This stimulation does depend, however, on the ability of those at the session to look at a new idea not in terms of its worth but in terms of what it can suggest. This is exactly the sort of attitude that was required for the random stimulation technique and it can be useful to practice this technique in order to develop the attitude. But even if this attitude has not been consciously developed, the stimulating effect of the group nature of a brainstorming session is useful.

The group structure has a disadvantage in terms of the tendency to evaluate ideas, and an advantage in terms of the interaction of ideas. There is a further bonus in the group structure. This is the tendency to show off, to try to dazzle others with the brilliance or novelty of an idea. This often takes the form of putting forward ideas which are so outrageous that they make the other members of the group laugh. Since such outrageous ideas can be very stimulating, the would-be comic can be encouraged rather than repressed.

Brainstorming as a formal envelope

A brainstorming session is a formal envelope. Within this envelope any of the techniques described in previous sections may be used. Picking out dominant ideas, tethering factors, and polarizing tendencies may be tried. Distorting, exaggeration, and reversal may also be used. Random words or objects can be introduced. The new functional word, PO (described in section 13), can be used, but this is not strictly necessary since the formality of the session already indicates the way ideas are being used. In a way, PO is a symbol or notation for the attitudes that should *already* be an automatic part of a brainstorming session.

Mechanics of a brainstorming session

Time. Most brainstorming sessions go on *too long*. Thirty minutes is the ideal time. Forty-five minutes is an outside limit. There is nothing worse than a brainstorming session which drags on in silence while the participants desperately try to think of something to suggest. The danger of boredom and of drying up is a real one, and if the technique is to be used as a routine it becomes very important that it should never be boring. Participants should look forward to a brainstorming session, not dread the agony of having to fill the time trying hard to think of ideas. Like a good meal, one should break off a brainstorming session when one has had not quite enough. It is better to cut off a session in the middle of a great flow of ideas than to linger on until the ideas dry up.

Warm-up period. If the participants are unfamiliar with the procedure or if they have not used it for some time, it is a good idea to have a warm-up session. This lasts for ten minutes and takes place immediately before the main session. For this warm-up session the problem ought to be simple and concrete; for example, design a better door handle or a toothbrush.

Number of people. The lower limit is six. Below that number it becomes an argument or a discussion. The upper limit is twelve. Above that number it tends to degenerate into a session where a few people talk and the rest serve as a silent audience.

Nature of the people. There should be a nucleus of people who are concerned with the problem (about one-third of those present) and the rest should be from as wide a range of interests as possible. This is easier to specify than to carry

119

out, for in practice the people usually belong to the same organization and are more or less concerned with the problem directly. Even so, an effort should be made to bring in people like accountants, personnel people, secretaries, and so on, as well as the more obvious creative people. It is important that the group should not contain anyone who is obviously senior to the others in the group. The presence of such a person can seriously inhibit the free flow of ideas. Though everyone knows that all sorts of mad ideas are acceptable, they cannot help feeling that they will be judged (at least subconsciously) on the practicality of the ideas they suggest. In practice, it may be hard to exclude a senior person from the group but it should be done. This stricture does not apply to organizations which are essentially creative (such as advertising agencies) for the senior people would appreciate the value of wild ideas.

Notetaker. The notetaker is kept so busy that he has little chance to put forward ideas of his own. On the other hand, the notetaking function is not simply a passive, secretarial one. The notetaker has to condense the ideas suggested and list them. This condensation is very difficult because, if it is too extreme, the actual worth of the idea may be lost. For example, the idea of using certain hours exclusively for transferring goods at high speed by rail might be put down as timesharing or timedistribution, which would not make much sense when the list was read later. On the other hand, there simply is not enough time to put down everything. Even if there were, it would still be necessary to condense the ideas so that from time to time the list could be read out in order to stimulate further ideas. In addition to the notetaker, a taperecording should be made of the session. This is not of much use during the session itself since it could only be played back in real time, but it can be used later to pick up ideas that were missed by the notetaker.

If the notetaker is not quite sure how to condense an idea, he can ask the person who presented the idea how it should be listed. The notetaker can also ask for a pause (or an assistant) if he cannot keep up with the flow of ideas. There is a strong temptation for the notetaker to leave out some ideas because he feels that they have been covered by ideas previously listed. Thus in the railway-lines problem the notetaker might leave out the suggestion of mobile libraries because he had already listed the idea of mobile shops. Yet the two ideas are different in the sense that they can lead to different further ideas. For instance, from the idea of mobile libraries might come the idea of mobile classrooms.

Duplicate ideas do get put forward in the course of a brainstorming session, but it is better to take the trouble to put these down than to decide what is a duplicate and what is not. After all, duplicates can be struck from the list later, but an idea which has been left out cannot ever be put back.

Chairman. The notetaker and the chairman are the only two people with any official function. The chairman's duties may be listed as follows:
1. To act as a lubricant to enable the session to proceed smoothly.
2. To stop everyone talking at once and give an opportunity to someone who has been trying to say something.
3. To define the problem at the start of the session and re- peat it at intervals throughout the session.
4. To stop people trying to evaluate ideas. The simplest way to do this is to use some standard phrase such as: "That is evaluation" or "I think you are evaluating".
5. To make sure that the notetaker has got the ideas down. He can ask for a pause in order to ensure this.
6. If the flow of ideas comes to an end, to ask for the note- taker to read out all the ideas so far listed.
7. To be ready with suggestions to put forward when the ideas of others dry up.
8. To start and stop the session, and to be responsible for its organization.

A good chairman can make a big contribution to the success of a brainstorming session, but a bad chairman can inhibit it. Some chairmen think their job is to organize the session, and they even go so far as to ask people in turn for their ideas. Such chairmen may try to get everyone to look at the problem in a particular way; for instance, "Let's all look at that door handle over there . . . ." A brainstorming session is *not* a cooperative effort in which everyone tries to produce an answer to the problem. On the contrary, it is an opportunity to generate as many different approaches as possible.

Definition of the problem. This is very important, for the actual definition used will directly determine the sort of ideas which are sparked. If the problem is defined too narrowly, one finds oneself thinking only of a specific way of carrying out some function. For instance, if the problem is to design a door handle then one thinks in terms of shape, material, and function. But if the problem is defined too broadly, one may find oneself in so large an area of consideration that useful ideas are rare. For instance, if the problem is defined as "the opening of doors", one might put forward ideas about doors themselves, gaps in the wall or the ceiling, protection devices, screens, sound proofing, and the like.

Unfortunately there are no easy rules to follow. If there is a specific problem to be solved, then the problem can be presented as such. If there is a general area for consideration (for example, a new cosmetic product), then it can also be presented as such.

Common errors. Certain attitudes or remarks occur with enough frequency in brainstorming sessions for them to be picked out and recognized—and then avoided.

- The major danger is evaluation. Some people find this very difficult to resist. There will often be one person in the session who (against his will) will find himself tending to evaluate. The chairman, or other members of the session, must be quite firm with their remark "That is evaluation".

- There will be a tendency to evaluate the novelty of an idea. This is more difficult to resist. The chairman can turn to the notetaker and say, "Never mind whether it is new or not—just get it down".

- The overworked notetaker will tend to leave out ideas by saying "We've got that down already under. . . ." Without an argument as to whether the new idea is really new, the notetaker should be asked to get it down.

- Participants in the session may wonder whether some of the ideas put forward are really relevant to the problem under consideration. There must be no question of the chairman, or anyone else, pointing out the irrelevance of an idea, for no idea is really irrelevant. The chairman can, however, counter the tendency to wander further and further from the problem by simply repeating the problem at intervals.

- With an inexperienced group, a lot of attention will be paid to the definition of the problem. Participants will spend time complaining that the problem is not defined exactly enough and that they are not exactly sure what they are supposed to be thinking about. At this point, the chairman states that they are not actually seeking a solution to a specific problem but seeking to generate ideas in the problem *area*. Thus the exact definition of the problem is not so important and anyone may treat it as it appears to him.

- There may be a tendency to treat the brainstorming session as a group analysis of the problem situation. This would involve dividing up the problem into parts, for instance, "Let us consider the functions of a door handle: first there is some means to grasp the door; second the handle serves to operate some latch mechanism; third. . . ." There is no easy way of cutting off this analytical attitude, but it can be very inhibiting for it carefully lays down the old way of looking at the problem instead of encouraging new ways. An experienced chairman would throw in some outrageous idea such as "I think handles should not be on doors at all but on the wall opposite."

- Some chairmen tend to dominate the proceedings too much. Ideas should not in fact be offered to the chairman but thrown out for the general benefit of the meeting and picked up by the notetaker. The chairman is only there to help things along, not to organize what should take place. If things are going well he should be invisible.

- Some people have such a fertile flow of ideas that there is little chance for others to speak. There is not much one can do about this (or would want to do about it) provided the flow is of different ideas. If the talk is only in terms of development of a single idea, the chairman should cut it off by saying: "We can put that down as. . . ."

- Participants are often uncertain whether they should sit and follow their own line of thought or listen to the ideas of others and develop them. There is no definite rule, both attitudes are necessary. One should listen to the ideas of others and not just wait for them to stop so that one can put up his own idea. One should now and then be in a position to say, "Carrying that idea further, why not have. . . ."

- Sometimes the ideas put forward may be rather humdrum and routine. When this happens, any experienced members at the session should liven it up by throwing in some wild ideas.

Follow-up

The minds of the participants in a brainstorming session are not automatically stopped when the session is ended. Ideas continue to arise even if no special effort is made to look for them. In order to catch these ideas which arise after the end of the session, it can be worth providing some sort of net. The simplest way to do this is to make copies of the list of ideas compiled by the notetaker and to send this along to each participant together with a blank sheet on which he is invited to list his latest ideas. The participants are asked to return the sheet immediately rather than hold onto it until they generate some further ideas.

Evaluation

The brainstorming session is followed up about a week later with an evaluation session. This can be made up of completely different people or can include some of those who took part in the original session. The usual methods of critical analysis, practicality, cost, et cetera, are used in the evaluation session. There is no need to go into these vertical thinking procedures in this book. The evaluating team can look at the list of ideas generated in the brainstorming session in the following way:

1. Pick out directly useful ideas.
2. Pick out ideas which seem worth exploring further.
3. Extract the functional aspect of even the wildest ideas.
4. List the different approaches used.
5. Note the ideas which can be tried out without difficulty.
6. Note the ideas which require more information before they can be accepted as feasible or rejected as impossible.
7. Note the ideas which have in fact already been tried out.

In one brainstorming session to discuss the retail distribution of detergents, it was suggested that they should be provided as from a village pump. Though this idea is in itself ridiculous one can easily extract the functional aspect which is to provide a neighborhood source, accessible at all times, and from which people would take according to their needs. From this one could easily go on to some sort of slot-machine bulk dispensing.

At the end of an evaluation session, one might draw up a list of ideas under the following headings:
1. Ideas for immediate use.

2. Ideas for further exploration.
3. Different approaches and attitudes.

Transcript of a brainstorming session

... This is the problem. Stamping prices in supermarkets is time-consuming and the problem is how to reduce it.

... The first idea is to have the manufacturer stamp the price on the goods—not necessarily a standard price but one dictated by whom they are selling to, a range of prices.

... You could use a standard manufacturer's price and let the supermarkets sell at whatever discount they liked.

... Issue a price list to the customer rather than having the price on the goods. The customer can consult his list.

... But that has a lot of disadvantages—

... Never mind about that

... Separate different goods to different cashiers—items under one dollar to one cashier, items over one dollar to another.

... The price is actually put on for the benefit of the cashier. You could have a whole pile of things like soft drinks with a little tag underneath showing the price to the customer, but it's the cashier who actually needs the price. You could overcome this by having more intelligent cashiers or by giving them a price list.

... Send cashiers to memory training courses.

... A paper strip could be attached to the goods and when the goods were handed to the cashier, she would just take the strip off and charge the price.

... Instead of taking goods, the people would just go round and make notes of what they wanted and then give this to the cashier. Then someone could put the whole order together as a load.

... You have a little credit card and you put this in. The shelf then opens up to deliver one of the items and stamps it.

... Stamps your card or a list?

... No, stamps the goods.

... The shelf would not open up until you put the card in.

... What we are looking at here is having all the goods stacked on shelves. If pricing is time wasting, then we could say, all right, don't put prices on. This is a start. So instead of the goods, you would only have one priced item as a sample and the goods would be kept in a warehouse. If you wanted an item like the sample you would press a button and this would extract the goods from the warehouse. All the items would be brought together for collection later.

... And pressing the button would automatically charge it on a bill, so you would not need to have a cashier at all.

... Yes, or the goods could be added up at the end.

... Carrying on from the credit card idea, if you don't want to carry a card around, there could be little bags of tokens which a person picks up as he enters a shop. He just puts one of the tokens on any goods he wants, but he doesn't bother to take up the goods. Then the goods identified in this way are collected and charged, and are waiting for him when he is ready to leave.

... This is a combination of the button-pressing system and the card system.

... That's right.

... You could have all prices as fixed multiples of basic units like pennies, nickels, dimes, and quarters. Then as you walked in you would be given a bag of these tokens, and to get something from the shelf you would have to drop in the right amount of tokens.

... A slot machine for tokens for all goods.

... Yes.

... You would buy the tokens at the beginning—or at the end by a calculation based on the number you have left.

... Would the goods be in a sort of box?

... On a shelf behind a glass door which only opens to the correct number of tokens.

... Meat is rather different because the weights are so variable.

... That is evaluating.

... No, just saying that perhaps one would have something different for the meat. Perhaps a weighing machine with a slot for tokens and you have to put in an amount that corresponds with the weight.

... Simple recording of purchases and then calculating prices overnight or at another slack period. Then send off bills of what people owe.

... An account system? People having accounts with super-markets.

... There are some goods like meat which are not really supermarket foods. You might say I want half a pound of this or a pound of that and the fellow puts it on the scale. The weight and the price could then be stamped at the same time.

... I think we ought to get back to the idea of making it easier for the cashier. Suppose there was a list with all the standard-price items on it and this was given to the shopper, who would mark off whatever goods he took. Then this card would be read by a machine with a mark-sensing device and there wouldn't even be a need for a cashier. Meat and extra items would be accounted separately.

... I think it is important to separate goods into those that can be handled by a mechanical system and those that might have to be handled in another way, instead of trying to devise an omnibus system that covers everything.

... Have separate cashiers, each one dealing with only one price, so all each one has to do is to count up the number of articles.

... You mean pricing by cashier rather than by goods?

... Not exactly. You just go to a different cashier for each price category and she just counts it up.

... Taking the credit card idea further, you could have a code number which you pressed opposite the goods you wanted, and then the goods could be all collected at the end under this code number and priced at the same time. This is just taking someone else's idea a step further.

... Can I catch up with a previous idea, the one with different priced girls? [laughter].

... You would have sections with single-price items in each. At the end of the section would be a cashier who just counted up the number of items.

... A sort of streaming effect.

... Yes.

... Elaborating that idea a bit further, in order to avoid having a huge range of prices, you would arrange with the manufacturers to have a small number of standard prices, say ten. And then, instead of varying the price, the manufacturers would vary the amount of goods put into the package. So instead of a variable price according to quantity, there would be a variable quantity in order to keep within fixed prices.

... You could do this for individual supermarkets that wanted to have a different size package to sell for the same price.

... You could also go over to measuring by weight or by size. The same size containers with variable amounts in them.

... Shouldn't we take cognizance of the facts of life in a

supermarket? I understand that adding a little bit to the price or taking a bit off is one of their stock-in-trade procedures. I don't doubt that it has some strong psychological reasoning behind it. As an outsider it seems to me that this is important to them.

... That is only possible because at the moment our monetary unit is so small. If we were to go over to a large basic unit, then this would no longer be possible. And life would be much easier for the cashier.

... Agitate for larger basic units of currency to cut out small price variations.

... This is the same as the token idea.

... Has anyone suggested making things up into unit-price packages? This way each package would cost the same price.

... Make the customer add up his own bill. Check all bills over a certain amount and sample ones below that amount.

... Attach a magnet tag to each article. This is added by a machine which can relate the pattern on the tag to the current price of the week.

... Can I restate the problem again. This is that the marking system, which is done by employees going around and stamping the prices on the goods, is time consuming. What we are asked to do is to think of ways to reduce that time.

... Get more work out of the staff.

... One could perhaps stick with the present pricing system but have automatic loading of the shelves with goods.

... Instead of having someone stamp each can, why not use a multiple stamp and stamp lots of cans at once?

... An automatic stamping machine within the supermarket rather than done by the manufacturer.

... Have a stamping machine on each shelf. There would be some stamped items and some unstamped, and as the number of stamped ones diminished a new lot would be stamped automatically by the machine.

... Perhaps the only way you could release a can from a shelf would be by pushing up a piston or something which had the price stamped on it.

... It's mighty hard not to evaluate.

... In other words you are shifting the onus of stamping from the girls to the customer.

... The customer can't avoid it.

... He's forced to do it because that's the only way he can release the item from the shelf.

... You could put your card into a slot, and as you took the goods out the price would be added to your total bill which would be waiting for you as you left. Or else you could carry the bill around with you. This way the price would be added for each item as you inserted the card into the slot.

... I want to concentrate on the time-saving aspect.

... Suppose we don't do any pricing at all.

... All items a common price.

... Or everybody gets charged an average amount.

... The average for the store would vary, either going up or down.

... No comment!

... It comes down to a matter of money, and cost of staff, things like that. But shouldn't we orient ourselves so that the systems we are proposing won't obviously be ten times as expensive as the ones we are replacing?

... I think if we do that we shall get on to evaluating very quickly.

... At the moment it is just a matter of getting ideas.

... But inwardly we reject an idea that is costly or impractical and we don't build upon it. That is why there has only been a small amount of cross-fertilization.

... It is very difficult not to evaluate. As each idea comes along you think, Oh Christ, that would never do.

... It's a matter of blocks, isn't it? I can't get out of my mind the idea that the poor bloody customer is going to be bossed around by a lot of these systems.

... Never mind about that.

... That may be but I can t stop myself from thinking that that would never work because . . .

... As long as you keep it to yourself that is fine for this purpose.

... But you will never try to build on that idea.

... You can't get enthusiastic about other people's impracticalities, even if you can about your own.

... Surely the whole idea is that if you see something impractical you can find a way around it instead of judging it and throwing it out.

... PO.

... I think if you have any faith in PO you should be thinking of it when you have these difficulties.

... Robots, you can stick that down.

... Have you any idea what they are going to do?

... Robot stampers, robot personnel.

... Do everything, do the whole lot, including the buying.

... A stamping device which had its own ink supply instead of having to be pressed onto a pad.

... What I meant by a mark-sensing device before was some way of putting a mark on the goods, magnetic or otherwise, so all the goods would be placed in front of a recorder which would add up the price automatically. This might eliminate the cashier altogether.

... So you are accepting the time wasting of stamping but you are trying to offset this by saving time elsewhere.

... The manufacturer could put on his price with the marker device and then as you read this off with your machine you could automatically apply your discount.

... I would just improve stamping equipment to save time.

... Supermarket staff seem to be very poorly motivated, and they actually do this job very slowly.

... Better motivation of staff?

... Stamp bonuses.

... Stamping competitions.

... Stamping with your feet while you are not doing anything else.

... If you are not doing anything else why not use your hands?

... But she is doing something else, she's the cashier.

... Get customers to do stamping and give them a bonus of free goods according to how much they did.

... Like dishwashing for your dinner.

... We don't have to use the whole thirty minutes, do we?

... No. If we have dried up, let's go over the list of ideas we have so far. Anyone who thinks his idea has been left out please say so.

Other formal structures

There are a number of other formal structures which encourage the generation of new ideas by providing a framework for the use of lateral thinking. The essence of these methods is that they provide a definite time, a definite communication setting, and a set of simple rules. In all of them there is some definite commitment to come up with new ideas that goes beyond a general vague intention to do so.

The structure may take the form of a simple sheet which is circulated to one person after another. Each recipient is asked to add to the sheet his own ideas on the problem defined at the top of the sheet (or on the top sheet of the pile). The sheet then moves on to the next person. In fact, the sheet is circulated twice so that the first person can be stimulated by the ideas of others which have been put down on the sheet after his own ideas on the first round. With this procedure, the ideas must always remain anonymous. If not, the ideas supplied will all be sound, sensible ones and no really new or provocative ideas will be forthcoming. No one wants to expose himself to the inadequate judgment of those who perhaps do not understand the process of creativity.

Another practical method involves the use of suggestion slips. This is not so much a formal structure for lateral thinking but an attempt to tap the ideas of employees. Each employee fills in a suggestion slip with an idea (one slip for each idea) and these are later collected and sorted out.

This book is, however, more concerned with the basic principles of lateral thinking than with particular structures for its use. The formal structures do have their uses but it is more important that skill in lateral thinking is developed by an individual and added to his ordinary thinking skill, rather than that he should be able to use some artificial technique on special occasions.

This section on the new functional word, PO, summarizes the whole book—and the entire concept of lateral thinking. If one understands the purpose and the use of PO then one understands the purpose and the use of lateral thinking. PO is a crystallization of the concept of lateral thinking. Thus PO is implicit in all the other sections on the nature and use of lateral thinking. Nevertheless, PO has been confined to this section because many readers may not be ready to go so far as to use a new functional word. Such readers may prefer to use the attitudes and general techniques of lateral thinking without being forced to use PO.

What is a functional word?

The best example of a functional word is NO and the whole concept of the negative which goes along with it. NO is the basis of acceptance or rejection. NO is the basis of the logical process of selection by exclusion of all that can be rejected. NO signals the mismatch between a possible idea and experience, and so gets the idea thrown out. Logic is the management of NO. Without the concept of the negative there could be no logic.

Just as NO is the basis of logical thinking, so PO is the basis of lateral thinking. Both words convey a way of dealing with ideas and information. Both words lack special meaning but indicate a function that is to be carried out. Both NO and PO could be called operational words.

The function of NO is to carry out the negative function. NO is the negative of language. The function of PO is to *laterate*. PO is the laxative of language.

PO as a tool

Lateral thinking can be carried on without an awareness of the principles of lateral thinking. Lateral thinking can certainly be carried on without the conscious use of PO. But as a practical tool, PO has many advantages.

● Instead of having to remember all the attitudes and

principles of lateral thinking one simply has to remember the use of PO.

● PO makes it much easier to teach lateral thinking as part of education, for one simply teaches the use of PO and all else follows.

● It is quite difficult to transfer a skill learned in one situation to new and different situations. This difficulty applies to the transference of the skill of lateral thinking from abstract situations to more realistic ones. But if one practises the use of a specific tool like PO, then this *tool* can be used in any situation just as a mathematical tool can be applied to any situation. This process is shown in Figure 13–1.

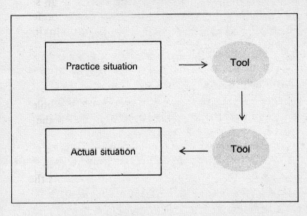

Figure 13–1.

● PO is useful as a formal indication that lateral thinking is being used. Otherwise there would be confusion if, for instance, a provocative statement made in a lateral fashion is understood in a logical fashion.

● PO is useful simply as a notation, as a formal shorthand.

● On the whole, people are terrified of introducing discontinuity into thinking. They are terrified of "negative" information steps. That is to say, steps that seem to create confusion rather than order. As a formal shorthand, PO makes it easier to use such negative information steps because they can be separated into "PO steps".

● PO does not carry with it any dogma, or belief, or even acceptance of a theory. PO is a neutral tool. PO is no more than an opportunity. No one should feel threatened by an opportunity. One uses PO as a tool, and if one does not find the tool useful one can stop using it. Moreover, the way the tool is used depends on how the person wants to use it. If you had a garden to be dug you could give someone explicit instructions as to how you would like it done—or you could show him how to use a hoe and then let him get on with it.

General function of PO

● PO is a-rational, not antirational.
● PO is an escape from the YES/NO system.
● PO is a fantasy device.
● PO is a repatterning tool.
● PO is an insight tool.
● PO is the laxative of language.
● PO introduces the discontinuity function.

PO may seem to be an anti-reason device, but it is not, because it works outside of reason and not in opposition to reason. A person in London may be speaking a strange language which is not understood by the people around him. This does not mean that the person is speaking anti-English but simply that he is speaking a *different* language, perhaps French. In the same way, PO does not work within the YES/NO reason system but is part of another system, the lateral thinking system.

The general function of PO arises directly from the behavior of mind as a patterning system. As discussed in a previous section, a pattern does not have a unique validity. A pattern is simply one way of putting together the information that has become available. The pattern reflects the sequence in which the information happens to have arrived. But the information itself can be put together in other and often better ways. Left to themselves, patterns tend to grow by continuity. This means that established patterns do not change but get added to. In order to restructure a pattern so as to put the contained information together in a new and better way, one must introduce some discontinuity. That is the function of PO: to introduce discontinuity into a patterning system. PO does not by itself bring about this restructuring (repatterning, rearranging) but PO provides a *step* toward it.

The YES/NO system is solely concerned with the correctness of the way information is put together. The YES/NO system is used to judge whether an arrangement of information is justified. Correctness and justification refer to whether the arrangement of information fits in with, or is compatible with, the patterns that have been established by experience. What is judged is not the validity of an idea, but whether that idea fits in with the pattern provided by experience. Since the pattern provided by experience has no unique validity, the YES/NO system assumes an arrogance it does not deserve. If one is trying to look for new ideas, it is no use trying to fit them into the old ideas. For this reason PO works outside the YES/NO system. PO is an escape from the YES/NO system. PO is a holiday from the YES/NO system.

With the YES/NO system the justification for putting things together is that they make sense (that is, they fit in with established ideas). With PO the only justification for putting things together is the possibility of what might happen next. One uses PO with an arrangement of information to see where it can lead. With the YES/NO system one must look back at the signpost to be sure he is on the right road. With PO one strides forward and then looks around to see if he has got somewhere useful.

PO implies: "Don't look for the logic behind this arrangement of information; instead let us go forward and see what the effect is." With PO one appears to do things without reason, but in fact the reason is what comes next. And in a patterning system there is a very good reason for introducing the discontinuity of the PO effect in order to bring about inside restructuring.

With PO one puts up an arrangement of information to see what happens. With PO one changes an arrangement to see what happens. In neither case is one doing it because it is *necessary* to do it. The necessity for doing it may arise only after an insight change has come about as a result of the rearrangement.

As a functional word, NO is used to weaken and destroy ideas which do not fit in with experience. PO is used to generate ideas *beyond* what is based on experience.

PO is never a judgment. PO is a request, a suggestion, an invitation, an indication.

Choice of letters

The letters PO were not chosen for any special reason. Another syllable could easily have been chosen. PO has no intrinsic meaning. It is the use of PO that creates its meaning.

The syllable PO is a strong and distinct sound, and is
sufficiently similar to NO to indicate its functional nature.
Furthermore, the syllable PO occurs in such words as:
hy*po*thesis
sup*po*se
*po*ssible
*po*tential
*po*etry
    All these words suggest the function of PO. *Hypothesis* and
suppose suggest a reasonable but unproved arrangement of
information. This is a very weak version of the PO function,
for PO can support a totally unreasonable arrangement of
information. *Possible* and *potential* are both concerned with
what might happen next, and this is another aspect of the
PO function. *Poetry*, like PO, is an arrangement of information in a provocative rather than an analytical manner.

Two basic uses of PO

PO really has but a single function and that is to generate
new ideas. There are, however, two aspects to this single
function. The first aspect is the provocation of new ideas.
The second aspect is the escape from old ideas. This second
aspect involves challenging the unique validity of any current
idea.
    These two aspects of the function of PO can be considered
as follows:
● To create provisional arrangements of information.
● To treat as provisional established arrangements of
    information.
    To use PO effectively, one must be aware of the usefulness
of patterns and at the same time of the arbitrariness of
patterns. One must be aware of the possibilities of generating
new patterns as well as the dangers of being imprisoned by
the old ones.

The first use of PO: Provocation

Evolution is supposed to proceed through change followed by
selection. Random mutation provides the change, and survival of the fittest provides the natural selection. The
evolution of ideas proceeds in a similar manner—but with a
very important difference. The random mutation process is
missing. The random mutation process is a totally unreason-

able one. There is no question of changing an animal species to make it more suitable for the environment, as is the process with ideas. The random change occurs and *then* it is found to be useful. So with the first function of PO, a provocative arrangement of information is made and *then* it may be found to be useful. If not, it disappears like all other useless changes.

Forward and backward use of information

Language and thought are used to describe what has happened, to explain how things came about, to show how something is compatible with past experience. Such analysis and description is a "backward" use of information. In the forward use of information one sets up an idea not for what it describes, but for what it can bring about. The difference between the two processes is suggested in Figure 13-2.

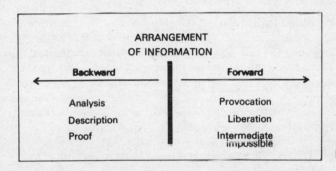

Figure 13-2.

The intermediate impossible

Faced with an idea, one rushes to judge whether it is correct or incorrect. If it is correct one accepts it and proceeds. If it is incorrect one throws it out and proceeds in a different direction. PO provides a third alternative which lies somewhere between acceptance and rejection. PO is not concerned with the validity of an idea but with its value in setting off further ideas. Thus an idea which would otherwise have been rejected at once may be saved for a while longer by the use of PO. PO does not reverse the judgment. PO does not make valid an idea which has been rejected as invalid. What PO does is to allow one to keep an idea under consideration *for a little while longer after it has been rejected.* That is to say,

137

instead of throwing it out at once, one keeps it a little longer, not forever.

Why should one want to hang on to an idea which can be properly rejected? The answer lies in the behavior of the patterning system of mind. In such a system, one may have to pass through an intermediate impossible stage in order to find a new way of looking at things. Three things can happen:

1. An idea may be judged wrong because it does not fit in with the current frame of judgment. But if the idea is held onto, the frame of judgment might itself come to change and the idea prove valid.

2. If an idea is held for a little while longer, it may spark several new ideas which would never have arisen if the idea had been thrown out at once. This is suggested diagrammatically in Figure 13–3. If the idea is rejected at

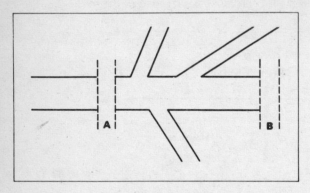

Figure 13–3.

point A, then no new lines of thought are opened up. But if the idea is rejected at B, new lines of thought will already have been started no matter what happens to the original idea itself.

3. It may be necessary to go through a "wrong" area in order to be in a position to see the right pathway. This is suggested in Figure 13–4.

In the first case the intermediate impossible may eventually turn out to be right after all. But in the second and third cases the intermediate impossible is wrong and remains wrong. An intermediate impossible is much more outrageous than an hypothesis or a guess. An intermediate impossible may be quite ridiculous.

There is another very important reason for encouraging the

138

use of the intermediate impossible. This is the shift of attention from *what is wrong with the idea* to *what is right with the idea.* The normal reaction is to try to find what is wrong with an idea so that it can be thrown out without further bother. By holding it as an intermediate impossible, one learns to extract all its usefulness even if it is to be rejected as a whole.

PO is simply put in front of an idea which is being held as an intermediate impossible. PO indicates that the idea is neither accepted nor rejected but is being held *as a stepping-stone to further ideas.*

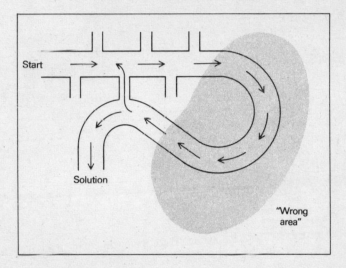

Figure 13–4.

In practice an intermediate impossible can be used in the following circumstances:

1. When presented by someone else with an idea which you are inclined to reject at once.
2. In the course of your own thinking when you come to an idea which is obviously wrong or impossible.
3. Deliberately setting up an intermediate impossible and seeing where it will take you.
4. Rescuing an idea which has already been firmly labeled with NO at some time in the past.

PO is usually an alternative to the judgment response of NO, but PO can also be used to temporarily override the NO label. This use of PO again sets up an intermediate impossible by allowing one to hold under consideration an idea which ought to be rejected—and in this case has in fact already been rejected.

Use of the intermediate impossible

In mathematics, $\sqrt{-1}$ is in a sense an intermediate impossible since it is impossible in itself but very useful for moving on to an answer.

Some young children were asked to design a dog exercising machine. One of the children came up with the idea of attaching a spring to each of the dog's feet (as shown in Figure 13-5) and then jangling the springs about. Quite

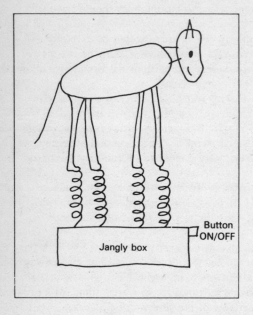

Button
ON/OFF

Jangly box

Figure 13–5.

obviously the child had mistaken the idea of movement for the idea of exercise. It would be quite wrong to suppose that the passive movements of the dog's legs would constitute exercise. And yet if one were to hold onto this idea as an intermediate impossible, one could come to a very interesting idea. If the movement of the springs had no rhythmic pattern and therefore could not be anticipated, the movement would actually be very good exercise even though it appeared to be passive. What would happen in fact is that the muscles in the legs would tense up to adjust to the current position, only to find it altering. Because of the physiology of muscles,

140

this would provide even better exercise than the popular (but dangerous in some cases) isometric method. Thus one passes through an apparently silly idea to end up with a good one.

In order to set up a deliberate intermediate impossible one can use the reversal method to turn things round, or one can use distortion or exaggeration. One can also deny the obvious. Or one can simply put forward the most ridiculous idea that occurs to one. The following examples of this process were obtained when a group of people were given a problem and an intermediate impossible, and then allowed just five minutes to generate ideas.

Problem: To reduce traffic congestion in cities.

Intermediate impossible: PO automobiles should have square wheels.

Ideas: Cars could not move—road would have to move—moving roadway would allow closer packing of cars as there would be no danger of collisions—it would also allow controlled circulation and speeds.

Square wheels—bumpy ride—make driving in cities unpleasant by taxation, or even just ridges in the road.

Square wheels—bumpy ride—ridges in the road with each bump registered by a meter in the car—motorist to pay meter charge (which would indicate his total usage of city roads).

Square-wheeled cars would have to use special roads—each automobile licensed to use certain city routes (indicated by color?)—fine imposed if found outside these routes.

Problem: To reduce supermarket thefts.

Intermediate impossible: PO all food should be given away free.

Ideas: Free food but entrance fee to store—standard fee calculated on turnover of the store week by week.

Free food for all with value totalled and distributed as a district tax.

Food club with membership card and charges based on total turnover—free food on showing of membership card.

Free discount on all purchases but amount of discount is reduced by theft losses for each week—hence shoppers keep an eye on fellow shoppers in order to preserve discount.

Food is free but pay for change in weight between entering and leaving supermarket—hand in weight ticket at weigh-out point.

Problem: Making railway passenger traffic more profitable.

Intermediate impossible: Passengers should be charged extra if their journey takes longer than scheduled.

Ideas: Such a charge would accelerate evolution of profitable routes—passengers would keep away from routes liable to surcharge and hence these unworkable services would be dropped.

Extra money on difficult routes would allow better equipment. Congested peak hour travel would be more expensive, which would encourage staggering of work hours in commuter areas.

Hidden charges for food and drink as journeys are lengthened. Charge for entertainment, not for journey—speed no longer an objective—cinema trains—television trains.

Always charge for occupancy time, not for distance or speed.

In each of the above examples the intermediate impossible seems to be a ridiculous idea. Nevertheless it serves to set off ideas which might be useful.

In using an intermediate impossible, the aim is never to try to show why the idea is not so impossible. The aim is always to use the idea as a stepping-stone to further ideas.

PO envelopes

There is usually an historical or logical reason for putting words together. "The secretary slammed the door" is an historical statement because that is what happened. "In times of inflation high interest rates are necessary in order to attract funds" is a logical statement because one can show how the two things are connected. Both types of statement are reasonable because both are true. One type describes an actual happening, the other type a logical reality. The statement "butterflies po frying pans" could conceivably be an historical statement if one were describing how some butterflies settled in a frying pan or if one were talking about a recipe for cooked butterflies. Otherwise the statement would be nonsense.

One of the functions of PO is to allow one to put together words or ideas in a way which would not be justified on any grounds. PO itself is the only justification. And the justification of PO is, as usual, that the arrangement can set off useful ideas. An artist might put together a frying pan and a butterfly in order to set off ideas of durability and fragility or solid usefulness and useless beauty.

Used in this way, PO does not connect the words in any way. PO provides an envelope for both the words. This envelope holds the words together in the same context. From this unnatural juxtaposition, ideas are set off. A juxtaposition is the simplest form of a PO envelope. For instance, one might take a random word from a dictionary and put it together with the problem under consideration in order to see what happened. (This procedure was discussed in a previous section.) PO is simply a convenient way of indicating what is happening, how the words are connected. A PO envelope has no communication value because it has no meaning. It has whatever meaning the arrangement of words happens to set off. And this would vary from person to person. The purpose of a PO envelope is stimulation, not meaning.

A PO envelope is more basic than an intermediate impossible because the latter is, after all, an idea even if a wrong one. A PO envelope can contain any arrangement of information. A juxtaposition is the simplest example, but the envelope may contain more than two things or even a mixture of objects and words.

PO can be used to hold together any arrangement of information whatsoever.

A catalyst (or an enzyme) serves to hold chemical molecules in such a position that they can link up with one another to form a new chemical. Without the catalyst the molecules would not link up. The catalyst does not itself form part of the new chemical. Once its holding function has proved effective, the catalyst drops away. PO acts like a special catalyst. It has a holding function to keep information in the same context or envelope. Then the information links together to set off a new idea.

Figure 13–6 represents a tube that is buried in the ground. The tube cannot be removed for examination. The problem is to measure the diameter of the constriction in the tube at point A. The vertical length of the tube is three feet and everything else is in proportion. This problem was given to a group of engineers, with five minutes in which to come up with ideas. They produced a number of routine ideas, some of them fairly adequate. Then PO was used to hold the word *spaghetti* in an envelope with the problem. The group was allowed an additional five minutes. Some of the ideas that came up are listed below.

Spaghetti—suggests filaments—push filaments down the

hole one by one until no more will pass through the constriction—diameter is then given by number of filaments used.

Spaghetti—filaments—use fiber optics with a camera at the end to actually photograph constriction.

Spaghetti—macaroni—tube—attach a small balloon to the tube and push through constriction in deflated state, then blow up balloon and try to withdraw tube—determine degree of inflation which will just allow withdrawal, then measure this diameter after withdrawal.

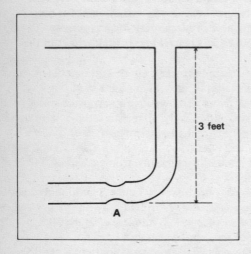

Figure 13–6.

Spaghetti is hard but becomes soft on cooking—use something soft which will harden and so give shape of constriction (for instance, a waxed loop which would be forced through constriction then harden to give impression)—perhaps a plastic foam with a catalyst, this would be poured in with a catalyst—plastic would foam up and set—it could then be withdrawn to give actual mold of constriction and this could be measured (such a foam does in fact exist and is used in medicine to obtain casts of colon growths).

There were several other similar ideas, including one based on the spaghetti hoop and using a circular deformation detector. Many of these ideas were quite sensible in themselves or as starting points for tackling the problem. Each of the ideas could have occurred without the introduction of "po spaghetti" but in fact they did not occur within the first period in which the problem was tackled.

On another occasion, a group of ten people were asked to consider the problem of car safety. They were given cards and asked to list all the separate ideas they had over a five-minute period. At the end of this period the cards were collected, but to their surprise the people were given another card and asked to write down more ideas in the next five minutes. At the end of the second five minutes the procedure was repeated yet again. The point was that the participants never knew they were going to be given more time so they did not hold ideas back. After three such periods, a random word picked out of a dictionary (the word was cheese) was introduced and a further five minutes was allowed for new ideas. The actual number of ideas produced in each five-minute period is shown in Figure 13–7. It is clear that in this

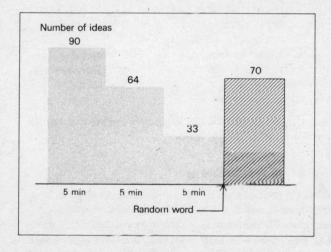

Figure 13–7.

particular case the supply of ideas was rapidly drying up. If the deadline had continued at the same rate, then without the introduction of PO the number of ideas might have been as low as 20. The introduction of PO and the random word more than doubled this.

Since so much of the labor force is employed directly or indirectly by the government, and since productivity in government service (as in all service industries) is slow to increase, one of the biggest opportunities for increasing output per man-hour in a nation's productivity is to increase productivity in government.

Taking a random word from a dictionary one can construct the PO envelope (or juxtaposition):
"Productivity in government po curtain."

Curtain—a visual barrier—make workings of government at all levels visible to taxpayers—also make workings of each department visible to other departments and to special efficiency panels.

Curtain—barrier to communication—improve communications—improve access to central recording facilities and so reduce duplicate work-recording systems.

Curtain—usually move from side to side to open and close—more people sideways through departments, not just up and down along the promotion ladder—give an increase in salary each time a sideways move is made.

A *curtain* can serve the function of a wall but is much cheaper—carry out extended functional analysis of government operations—can apparently essential functions be carried out in a simpler and cheaper way?

Curtain—hangs not from one point but from several—remove hierarchical bottlenecks which slow things down—have decentralized parallel organizations which interact directly with one another.

This sort of operation is the same as that carried out with the introduction of a random word.

The second use of PO: Change

The second use of PO is to treat as *provisional* ideas which are regarded as definite. The natural tendency of the mind is to regard established ideas as absolutely correct. PO is used as a reminder that the ideas may be correct in terms of the pattern that has been set up by experience, but that this pattern itself is an arbitrary arrangement of information which can be looked at in other ways.

PO is never a judgment. PO is outside the YES/NO system. PO does not affirm or deny. PO in its second function is used to challenge arrogance and dogmatism. PO does not challenge the correctness of a statement but it does challenge the *uniqueness* of that point of view. It is the fixity or rigidity of an idea that is challenged by PO, not the content of the idea.

In challenging the uniqueness of an idea as the only way of putting information together, PO is used to suggest that other ways might be found if one started *looking*. PO is used

146

to suggest such a search for alternatives, for different ways of looking at things, for different ways of putting things.

If you cannot find fault with a statement, then you must accept it within the YES/NO system. Yet you may be unhappy with the statement. You may be unhappy with the statement not because of any error in the way the basic concepts are linked together, but because you do not accept the uniqueness of the basic concepts themselves. The YES/NO system shifts attention from the basic concepts themselves to the way they are handled. PO is a device to challenge the uniqueness of the basic concepts. In many arguments, the conclusion is already determined by the concepts with which one starts—it hardly matters what happens in between. PO is used to ask for *a change in the basic concepts*.

By challenging uniqueness of a point of view, PO is in effect asking for a change. This change is for the sake of change. It is not a change because something is wrong or because something cannot be understood. PO asks for an alternative way of putting things, for an alternative way of looking at things.

In effect PO says: "I accept that, without judging it, as a particular way of looking at things—but let us try to find another way of looking at them." The person who made the original statement that is being challenged by PO tries to find another way of looking at things which makes sense to him. It is not a matter of his having to accept the other person's point of view. It is enough that he finds an alternative way of looking at things. This alternative is not a substitute for the original way but a new way to be put alongside the old.

The purpose of this change is to escape from the fixity of the old pattern and so come up with a new one. Once the possibility of change has been introduced, one is very likely to reach a conclusion that is different from the original one. Since a concept exists only insofar as it has a unique meaning, a sideways change of concept to an alternative one will no longer carry exactly the same meaning and this means that ideas are free to develop in a new way.

Focusing

PO can be applied to an entire statement or even to an entire argument. PO can be applied to a phrase, a sentence, a paragraph, an article, a book, or a policy. PO indicates that it is one way of looking at things but not the only possible way.

PO can also be used in a more precise manner by being focused on a single concept. When it seems that a whole point of view depends on the rigidity with which a single concept is held, PO can be applied to that concept as an invitation to change it.

Consider the following statement:

"Incentive selling is the only way to get the best out of a salesman."

PO could be applied to the statement in a variety of ways.

The simple response "PO!" This applies PO to the whole statement, to the whole idea. This use implies that the statement is accepted as a particular point of view but not as having a unique validity.

"PO incentive selling." This might be met by the response: "Selling on commission. Prizes or awards to best-performing salesman. Some means whereby a salesman's efforts are directly rewarded in proportion to those efforts." This particular use of PO moves one away from the word *incentive*, which begs the question by implying something which gets a salesman to work harder. By changing this to the idea of rewarded effort, one can move on to other ideas such as sales records and direct promotion.

"PO only way." This might be met by the response: "It is the most effective way. It is the one to which most of them respond." This might lead to consideration of what other ways had been tried or how badly the other ways had failed. It might also lead to whether salesmen in different countries respond in the same way. It might even lead to the idea that a company using incentive selling only attracts salesmen who prefer this form of activity, and that potentially valuable salesmen who dislike this method go elsewhere. If that was the case, then it was no wonder that the salesmen did respond to this method.

"PO get the best out of a salesman." This might be met by the response: "Make him reach his maximum selling ability. Put up the volume of his sales." This could lead to consideration of whether high-volume sales are necessarily good sales. Are such sales repeatable or once-only shots? Is the technical back-up to service these sales available? Does a salesman who sells in high volume necessarily sell well? Is volume the only factor? Is intermittent high volume better than a steady average volume? Is incentive selling capable of getting the individual best out of each salesman or only of getting a standardized concept of best out of all of them?

"PO best." This might be met by the response: "Best for the company." This would lead to such considerations as whether what is best for the company is also best for the salesman, for the buyer, for society in general.

Used in this focused way, PO makes one pause and look again at a concept instead of gliding over it and assuming its unique validity.

Response to PO

The response to the first use of PO is not so important. It is enough to appreciate that the arrangement of information covered by PO is provisional and meant to be *stimulating*. It is the person using PO who actually goes on to generate the ideas. But with the second use of PO, the response is more important since it is the person to whom it is addressed who must respond. Since PO is never a judgment, the response must never be a defense of the original way things were put. There is nothing to defend. Nor should one repeat the statement with exasperation and maintain that there is no other way of putting things. PO is an invitation to put things in a different way. Even if this different way is not so good as the original way it should still be used. It may be that the person making the original statement cannot think of another way of putting things. In that case the person using PO can try to help him find a way. PO invites a *cooperative* effort, not a competitive one.

Escape from names, labels, classifications

Names, labels, and classifications are all very useful. But they *fix* a particular way of looking at something. The word *cup* immediately unites all drinking vessels other than those made of glass. One looks at the object in terms of its drinking function. By saying "PO cup" one tries to escape from this way of looking at it in order to consider it as table furniture, as art, as an object which is comfortable to hold, as a container. "PO Operations Research" shifts the emphasis from someone who has training and background in OR to general problem-solving ability, to which are added such specific techniques as linear or dynamic programming. Instead of OR consisting of a bundle of techniques, these are reduced to the status of tools. In these circumstances PO implies: "Let us look at this in a way *other* than the usual way."

The third use of PO: Pause

It was stated earlier in this section that there are two aspects of the use of PO: the provocative arrangement of information, and the challenging of an arrangement in order to bring about a change. The third use of PO has to do with passing from one idea to another. PO provides a pause. As usual PO introduces a *break* in the continuity.

A person insults you. The natural reaction is to insult him back. Action is followed by reaction. PO is introduced as *a neutral reaction which means nothing*. It is not possible to delay a reaction with a real pause. One cannot have a gap. The gap must be filled with something. PO is definite enough to fill the gap and yet it has no meaning. In this way PO introduces discontinuity between one part of a pattern and its continuation.

The more obvious a reaction, the more easily it follows the action which sets it off. So quick is this continuation that other alternative reaction patterns have no chance. By introducing a neutral gap, PO makes it possible to move away from the obvious reaction and perhaps to use another. Anger and fury are immediate and usually blind reactions. If one can but hold them off for a while, one can move to more useful reactions. In a similar way, one idea may answer another with a direct inevitability. It is only by introducing a device like PO that one can weaken this inevitability. PO interrupts the action/reaction vicious circle. By breaking the continuity, PO provides an escape.

This particular use of PO is quite simple. Just as PO was used to hold off the rejection of an idea, so PO can be used to delay the obvious response to an idea. The purpose of this delay is to allow other responses to come forward. Once the obvious response has been made it is impossible to go back and consider alternative responses. The more obvious the response the more it needs to be delayed.

This process is shown in Figure 13–8. Normally the first idea is immediately followed by the response idea. The alternative ideas never get a look in. The insertion of PO *holds off* the obvious idea and allows exploration of the others.

This pause use of PO could also be regarded as a blocking

150

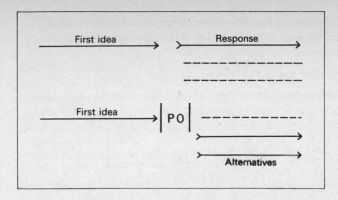

First idea → Response →

— — — — — — — —

— — — — — — — —

First idea → | PO | — — — — — — —

→

→

Alternatives

Figure 13–8.

use. PO may be regarded as temporarily blocking the obvious pathway.

Neutral response

This pause function of PO can be used not only to intercept action and spontaneous reaction, but it can be used as a response itself. Instead of responding to a situation with the limited choice and the commitment of YES or NO, one can simply say PO. What this means is, "I hear you". This particular use of PO can be confused with the interjection of PO to indicate that a particular point of view does not have an absolute validity. The same difficulty arises when YES can mean agreement or a simple acknowledgment that the message has been heard.

Grammatical use of PO

Since PO is a word, it needs to have some position among other words. The rules for placing PO are simple. There are three basic positions:

1. PO may be used by itself as an interjection. Used in this way it can mean one of two things: either a neutral noncommittal response or an invitation to change the way something has been put. In effect, PO used by itself implies: "That is one way of looking at things."
2. PO may be used directly in front of a word, a phrase, a sentence, or a statement. Here it implies that the arrangement of information is provisional. This may involve the provocative arrangement of the first use of PO or the change challenge of the second use.

3. PO may be used between words or in front of words to indicate a PO envelope which holds together information that would otherwise not hold together.

The practical use of PO

The various uses of PO may appear different but they are all aspects of the same thing. The essential function of PO is to introduce discontinuity into a patterning system. In practice, one would probably make use of only one or another function of PO. For instance, you may use PO to support an intermediate impossible. Someone else may use it as a neutral response. In time, one might get used to all the various uses of PO and even invent new ones. After all, there are a variety of ways in which NO and the negative are used.

Symbolic function of PO

Even if the actual word PO is never used in language or in thought, it serves a useful purpose as a *symbol* which indicates the nature of lateral thinking. To understand the use of PO is to understand lateral thinking.

● PO is a crystallization of the principles of lateral thinking.
● PO is a tool for language and thought. It is not easy to transfer a skill from one situation to another but one can transfer the use of a tool.
● Once a formal tool exists one can develop skill in its use.
● PO bears the same relationship to lateral thinking that NO bears to logical thinking.
● PO is a neutral operational word. It has no meaning but it allows one to use information in a lateral way in order to bring about new ideas.
● PO is a formal notation to show how information is being used. Without such a device there would be confusion.
● PO may be used in one's own thinking or in communication with others.
● Even if one never uses PO in a formal manner, a knowledge of the way in which it is used can make one's thinking more lateral.
● Teaching the use of PO is a convenient way of teaching lateral thinking.
● PO is an insight restructuring tool.

- PO is an opportunity. It carries with it no dogma.
- As with lateral thinking the use of PO may or may not prove useful in a particular situation, but the ability to use PO should increase the chances of escaping from old ideas and generating new ones.

There are a number of ways of obtaining creativity:
1. Borrow new ideas from others. Wait for other people to develop the ideas and then adopt them, copy them, use them as inspiration, or buy them.
2. Use an outside creative agency to develop new concepts. Buy as much creativity as is needed when it is needed or on a routine basis.
3. Employ creative people, consider creativity an important factor when selecting employees. Choose the creative people already employed and give them opportunities and encouragement.
4. Train people to be more creative.

If one were simply looking for new ideas, the first two methods would probably be the most effective. They do have the disadvantage, however, that they do not make special use of the knowledge, experience, or opportunities that are available within an organization. Method 3 would overcome this limitation.

But creativity is not simply a matter of looking for new ideas. It is also knowing when to look for new ideas, reacting to them, and developing them. More important than the generation of new product ideas is the creativity involved in change. This is the creativity involved in bringing ideas up to date, in being able to look at things in different ways. This is the creativity involved in problem solving and in dissatisfaction with merely adequate ways of doing something.

One can delegate the generation of new product ideas, but one cannot delegate the other aspects of creativity because they can never be isolated from all other business activity. Creativity is not a special need for special purposes. It is an integral part of thinking.

Creativity through the use of lateral thinking

In order to use creativity as an integral part of thinking, one employs the techniques and attitudes of lateral thinking. It is true that some people will make more use of lateral thinking than others. It is also true that some jobs require more lateral thinking than others. But some degree of skill in lateral thinking is essential for anyone who wants to use creativity as part of thinking.

Lateral thinking is not just a method for the R&D department or the OR problem solvers. Nor is lateral thinking restricted to those who show an especial interest in it. In a way, it is the people who do not appear to need lateral thinking in their work (for example, line administration) who need it most since R&D and marketing people will already be aware of some of the principles of lateral thinking. Similarly, it is those who are least enthusiastic about the idea who could most benefit from it, since the lack of enthusiasm often covers a tendency toward rigid, dogmatic thinking.

Talent

Some people use a form of lateral thinking anyway—but usually in a rather haphazard manner. They rely on chance to set off ideas rather than trying to do anything deliberate about it. Other people obviously have a natural aptitude for lateral thinking, just as some people have a natural aptitude for humor or for mathematics. The existence of such talent does not mean:
1. That such people do not need training in lateral thinking.
2. That other people cannot be trained in lateral thinking.

A person with a natural talent for lateral thinking will have this talent much enhanced by training in lateral thinking, just as a person with natural ability in mathematics will benefit more than other people from a training in mathematics. On the other hand, such training should not be restricted to those with a natural talent for lateral thinking. After all, one would not dream of teaching mathematics to only those with natural ability in the subject.

Creative brilliance is admirable, but it is not the most useful sort of creativity. Mathematical brilliance is admirable, but most of the usefulness of mathematics lies in the ordinary workaday application of this mental tool. Training in lateral thinking is not going to turn everyone into a creative genius. On the whole, the emergence of the occasional creative genius is much less important than a modest rise in creativity all round. The purpose of training in lateral thinking is to make available to everyone some skill in creativity—not to produce the creative genius who ought to produce himself. Effectiveness is what matters, not the occasional sunburst of brilliance.

Stages in training

The different stages in lateral thinking training (or any other training) could be listed as follows:
1. Interest
2. Understanding
3. Practice
4. Skill
5. Use

Interest and understanding together provide the background. They also determine the attitude towards lateral thinking. This attitude determines the amount of skill that will be developed and the useful application of this skill.

Background and attitude

The four most harmful attitudes are:
1. Apathy ("We have managed all right without it so far.")
2. Intense enthusiasm ("This is great, this will solve all our problems.")
3. Know-all ("I have always thought like that anyway.")
4. Defensive resentment ("It's a new fad that will pass.")

To some people, lateral thinking is perfectly natural, even obvious. To others, it appears "ridiculous", "gimmicky", "dangerous", or "confusing".

Gimmick

Some of the techniques of lateral thinking (and even the new word PO) can easily be seen as gimmicks. This hardly matters if these "gimmicks" are used often enough to become habits of thinking and eventually useful thinking tools.

The logic of illogicality

It is possible for one to find lateral thinking a beneficial empirical procedure without bothering with the underlying reasons for using it. Although acceptable, this attitude prevents one from really understanding the nature of lateral thinking and applying it as more than a particular technique of limited usefulness.

The most satisfactory approach is to go into the broad behavior of patterning systems, and to show that in such systems some method of introducing discontinuity is essential if one is to update old ideas and to develop new ones. Lateral thinking has a perfectly sound system basis. On the surface it may appear illogical, but one can work through a logical process to show why this illogicality is necessary. As soon as one understands this necessity for lateral thinking, he no longer has to regard it as a useful but crazy procedure. He no longer needs to be apologetic about it.

There is nothing difficult about the patterning behavior which underlies the need for lateral thinking, and it is better to use this approach rather than to put forward lateral thinking as a strange creative technique which seems to be useful in practice. This system approach also explains that lateral thinking is not really anti-reason but that it is in fact based on reason. With this approach the commitment to lateral thinking is one of understanding rather than emotional appeal.

Luxury

Lateral thinking may seem a luxury to be added to one's other thinking tools if one has time to attend to it. In fact, lateral thinking is not something to be added to one's ordinary thinking procedures but something that ought to come before them. The importance of lateral thinking as a part of ordinary thinking is shown if one emphasizes the clear distinction between the first and second stages of thinking. The first stage is the perceptual patterning stage, which is concerned with the way of looking at things, the choosing of concepts. The second stage is concerned with the processing of these concepts. By carefully distinguishing between the first and second stages, one sees the necessity for lateral thinking. One also sees that lateral thinking does not diminish or interfere with the second-stage thinking techniques. This reassures those people who feel that any skill they acquire in lateral thinking will interfere with their vertical thinking and confuse them.

Training methods

These will be considered under the following headings:
1. BACKGROUND
2. GROUP PRACTICE
3. INDIVIDUAL PRACTICE

Background

1. Reading material. The most direct way would be to give copies of a book such as this to all those who were to be trained. One could use a simpler book such as *New Think* (Basic Books, N.Y.)* but this provides only a general approach to lateral thinking. It would be better for the people involved to have copies of this present book rather than just to read it and pass it along. The book can then be used as a reference background in the training course. It is a bad idea to extract bits from the book and to circulate these, because such selection is apt to give a distorted and gimmicky view of the subject.

2. Seminars and lectures. Executives can also develop a background by attending one of the several courses organized by creative consulting agencies. Most of these agencies favor one or other particular technique which uses the basic principles of lateral thinking in a special format. There is a danger in this approach: Concentrating on one technique tends to obscure the basic nature of lateral thinking and reduce it to the use of that particular technique. The other difficulty is that it is often impractical to send all executives to such courses. It must also be remembered that such courses provide only a background or initiation into the subject, and that unless the ideas put forth in the courses are practiced on a regular basis the effect of the course is lost.

The other alternative is to arrange for an in-house seminar to be given by someone experienced in lateral thinking. There is no need for such a person to come from outside if there is already within the organization someone who has experience in and knowledge of the subject. But there is little use in sending a person on a course and expecting him to come back and pass on his newly acquired knowledge. All that person would be able to pass on would be the simple catch-phrases; he could not pass on the basic attitude and experience which only arise from having worked in the field.

* *The use of Lateral Thinking* (Jonathan Cape, London).

It is this experience that is so important in teaching lateral thinking, because it consists in knowing the difficulties which different people have in handling lateral thinking. This is not something that can be passed on through mere exposure over a short period.

If it is decided to provide a background by getting the executives to read a book such as this, it is not a good idea to ask for comments or to arrange a special session in which the material is to be discussed. By asking for comments, one encourages the reader to fix his attitudes at too early a stage. In this exploratory stage it is harmful to force people to form their attitudes because they will ever afterward be guided by those fixed attitudes. Anyone who is asked for comments on a subject finds it essential to pick out aspects or points with which (at his present state of knowledge) he disagrees. At this stage such disagreement hinders rather than helps, for a person has no obligation to use that part of the process with which he disagrees. On the other hand, points which are not clear can be discussed at the group sessions described below.

Group practice

The main purpose of setting up group practice sessions is to provide a definite framework for training in lateral thinking. The discipline of having a definite time and place for the training is much better than leaving it to an individual to choose his own training time as and when he wishes. The practice sessions need not be very long or very frequent. Weekly or monthly one-hour sessions would be ample.

The size of the group is not critical but, in order to allow interaction between the group and the leader, 30 people should be regarded as a maximum number.

The group is not a general discussion session like a brainstorming session since that is not a particularly effective form of training. There is a group leader whose task is to make himself thoroughly familiar with the point to be considered at the session, and then to explain this to the others, allowing time for examples, practice, and discussion.

It is important not to try to cover too much at any one session; this can be confusing and even boring, as people lose the point of what is being done. One or two points at each session is enough. These points can be obtained by working through this book using the sections on techniques and also the sections on the pattern behavior of the mind.

Below are examples of the sort of points that can be made the basis of a group practice session.

- Picking out the dominant idea, tethering factors, polarizing tendency. This could be based on a circulated report, on a newspaper article, on a presentation made to the group by one of the members on some subject.
- QUOTA. Filling a quota of different ways of looking at a situation. Discussion of the ways chosen.
- Use of the random word technique.
- Introduction of PO. Use of PO to generate intermediate impossibles.
- Brainstorming sessions. For these, the large group would divide up into smaller groups.

To begin with, the problems used for practicing lateral thinking should not be derived directly from the firm's activities. This is to prevent those taking part from being bogged down in policy details and practical considerations. Once some skill in lateral thinking has developed, the problems can be real and of immediate interest.

The sessions should be enjoyable rather than intense, and, in fact, could come to provide a free-thinking holiday for executives who had to spend the rest of their time on analytical activities. An essential part of the sessions is that the participants are made to consider problems other than those they normally handle. Thus accountants might find themselves considering marketing problems, and production managers might find themselves considering personnel problems.

The purpose of the sessions is not so much to train people in lateral thinking as to get them going. The basic idea is that after each session those taking part should continue to practice the particular method demonstrated. Certain methods, like brainstorming, are essentially group methods, but most of them involve attitudes of mind and things which can be developed in the course of one's own personal thinking.

Circulating sheets

As an adjunct to the group practice sessions, duplicated sheets can be circulated as a practice method for lateral thinking. For instance, a sheet might carry a problem and an intermediate impossible; the task would be to generate some

160

ideas and return the sheet with the ideas noted on it. Another sheet might contain a report, and here the task would be to pick out the dominant idea.

Unless the distribution and collection of these sheets are well organized, however, no one may bother to fill them in. Another danger is that the executives may feel that the sheet constitutes some on-going *test* of their creativity. To prevent this, the completed sheets need not be signed. Although anonymity would reduce the return flow, someone could be made responsible for collecting the sheets from a group of colleagues.

At no time should the problems chosen be so boring that filling in the sheets becomes a chore.

Groups and individuals

Modern training methods often use small groups or syndicates to examine a problem and suggest a course of action. It is natural to try to apply this group procedure to lateral thinking, but there is a danger in this. The purpose of a group is to arrive at a well-reasoned and worked-out point of view which is acceptable to everyone in the group. Lateral thinking, on the other hand, is concerned with generating *different* points of view. Groups tend toward *average* or compromise solutions, whereas lateral thinking seeks to encourage the extreme *individual* point of view. There is the added problem that, in a group situation, the more inhibited members may put forward only the reasonable ideas which they know to be acceptable to the others.

It is best to start off with the generation of individual ideas. For instance, after watching a short film of a salesman in action the group would not be asked to discuss it as a group. First, each individual would commit his own ideas to paper. The pieces of paper would be anonymous but the ideas on them would be read back to the whole group. In this way, the members of the group would be made aware of the ideas of the others—and so induced to wonder why they had not thought of that approach themselves. After this individual generation of ideas, the situation could be discussed in a group situation. The ideas derived from the individuals could be evaluated or elaborated and new ideas added.

Group situations can be stimulating but, basically, lateral thinking is an individual matter.

Individual practice

The purpose of individual practice in lateral thinking is to acquire skill and confidence in this type of thinking. The confidence is more important than the skill. The usual mistake is to spend too much time trying out lateral thinking. The amount of time spent in practice is not nearly as important as the frequency with which a little time is spent.
Individual practice can take two forms:
1. DELIBERATE USE OF LATERAL THINKING
2. REACTION USE OF LATERAL THINKING

Deliberate use. This implies setting out to practice a lateral thinking procedure. For instance, one might pick a word out of a dictionary at random and, holding it in a PO envelope with the problem, spend about three minutes seeing what ideas are triggered off. This short three minutes may be all the time spent on lateral thinking that day. Another time, one may find oneself reading a magazine article and may decide to pick out the dominant idea (tethering factors, polarizing tendencies, et cetera). This can be done either by writing these things down on a separate piece of paper or, more simply, by underlining those phrases in the article which seem to embody the points selected.

Another practice technique is to take a problem, generate an intermediate impossible, and then see what ideas follow. A variation is to take the way something is done at the moment, turn it around (reversal), and see where one can get to.

One could also attach PO in its change/challenge function to some basic concept used in a line of argument (as in the lead article in a newspaper) and restructure the concept to see what happens.

When one finds a problem or a situation looked at in a particular way, one could try quite deliberately to fill a quota (3 or 4) of different ways of looking at that situation.

Most of the techniques described in the previous sections can be practiced in this way. Some of them will prove easier to use and will be more enjoyable. In time one may select a favorite. The important thing to remember, however, is that one is practicing not a particular technique but lateral thinking in a particular embodiment.

It is important not to spend too much time practicing lateral thinking or trying to get a technique to work. The amount of time does not matter. Quality is what matters. Three to five minutes a day of free lateral thinking is quite enough—and better than hours of hard trying. It does not matter whether the techniques work or not. It is easy to be disappointed because a three-minute use of a random word does not turn up a brilliant new idea. In time success and confidence will come. It is better to stop after three minutes and feel that one could have gone on than to go on and find that nothing happens.

Reaction use. For the majority of people this is the most important use of lateral thinking. Not everyone is in a position where he is called on to generate new products. Not everyone has problems which have to be solved in a creative way. Not everyone feels the need to sit down and be creative. The "reaction use" of lateral thinking is when one uses lateral thinking to *react* to a situation rather than to generate a situation.

It may be a matter of stopping oneself from rejecting an offered idea immediately. One can see why the idea can be thrown out but uses PO (mentally) to hold on to the idea to see where it can lead. PO may also be used in its challenge/change capacity to react to an argument or line of thought. PO implies that you accept the idea as being valid for the person putting it forward, but challenge its absolute validity. PO may also be an invitation to escape from a particular concept prison. "PO truth . . . that which when found would relieve one of the necessity for looking for it." PO may also be used as a neutral response or pause to stop oneself from reacting to an idea with the immediate and obvious response.

All these uses of PO involve a certain effort until they become automatic and turn from an activity into an attitude. The word PO does not actually have to be expressed aloud for one can use it mentally to bring about the same effect. Alternatively, one can actually say "PO" and then explain what it means. When the other person is familiar with the use of PO it is more convenient to use it. But the attitude can be there whether or not one makes use of the word.

Responsibility for training

Who should undertake responsibility for training in creativity and lateral thinking? It may be someone who has a special interest in this area, but it is dangerous to allow the subject to become the private property of a small enthusiastic group as this tends to put other people off. Ideally, it should be someone with research responsibility—someone who has that necessary combination of practical effectiveness and an understanding of the creative process. A highly creative person is not very suitable as it will always seem that his creativity is innate and has nothing to do with his proficiency in lateral thinking. Nor might such a person have the necessary perseverance and patience with less creative colleagues.

There is no reason why training in lateral thinking should be treated any differently from other sorts of training. For instance, if there is a training officer in the organization he should be responsible for this training. The whole purpose of lateral thinking is to remove the mysticism from creativity and to make it available as a skill which can be learned and practiced like any other skill. It is not inspiration that matters so much as understanding and practice.

Lateral thinking is difficult to learn

Lateral thinking is not at all easy to learn for several reasons:
1. Lateral thinking contradicts many of the traditional habits of thinking which have been established by education (for instance, the need to be right all the time; the analytical use of information).
2. Lateral thinking is unnatural insofar as the natural tendency of the mind is to create and maintain rigid patterns.
3. Lateral thinking encourages open-ended ambiguity and many people are made unhappy by such insecurity (for example, there may not be a reason for saying something until after it has been said).

Danger of enthusiasm

In lateral thinking training, initial enthusiasm can be harmful. The idea may be seized upon as a new fashion and dropped when it is no longer new. The idea may be seized upon as some special technique by those who have found they have nothing else to offer and are therefore looking for a new source of importance. The idea may be overworked to the extent that it is tried on every possible occasion until everyone is fed up with it. The idea may be regarded as some magic formula that is going to work by itself—when the formula is applied and no brilliant answer is forthcoming, disappointment sets in.

It is much better to treat lateral thinking quietly, almost as a routine procedure. Gradually one comes to acquire skill and confidence in its use. Lateral thinking is a necessary part of thinking—not used instead of other thinking procedures but alongside them. Because lateral thinking is largely neglected in education and training, it comes to have a new and exotic appearance, which does it more harm than good.

The opposite danger is when people feel that they have always used lateral thinking and therefore have nothing to learn. People who make this claim usually tend to have too high a regard for their own creative ability. Those who do in fact have a high creative ability are the first to see the point of lateral thinking and to use it deliberately. Since they already understand the processes, they are eager to be able to use them deliberately instead of being dependent on chance happenings. Too often, the person who "knows everything" has the knack of being able to see in things only that small part with which he is already familiar.

Problem solving/design/innovation

In practice, problem solving, design, and innovation are very different things—so much so that they are usually dealt with by different departments and different people. An operations research team might try to solve a problem. The R&D department would be concerned with innovating new products. Design might be contracted out to a specialist. Yet the basic process involved in all three activities is the same.

All three processes have the same endpoint-effectiveness. Since there may be different degrees of effectiveness, the practical endpoint is satisfaction. This satisfaction point may be definite if the objective is to bring about a certain specified effect (for example, a mathematical problem for which an answer is produced). Or the endpoint may be arbitrary and defined by the personal satisfaction of the person who is tackling the situation or whoever has asked for the situation to be tackled. It may be the designer who is happy or the person who has ordered the design. Ideally one would like to show effectiveness in real terms such as market reaction to a new product, but in most cases the process (problem solving, design, or innovation) has to stop at some temporary point and be judged in terms of how useful it *might turn out to be.*

The interchangeability of the three processes is shown by the following phrases:

"We have a design problem here."

"We need to design a solution for this problem."

"There is need for a really innovative design."

"The problem is to design a new product which will make full use of our marketing facilities."

In practice the difference between the three processes is given by the degree of definition of the starting point and the endpoint.

● In problem solving the starting point and the endpoint are clearly defined. The problem is either to link up this starting point to the endpoint or else to change things so as to get rid of the conditions to be found at the beginning. For instance, the problem may be to reconcile a new wage claim with production costs. Or the problem may be to deal with an inefficient manager. Or it may be to find the communication bottlenecks in an organization.

● In design the starting point may be well defined or only loosely defined. It may be a matter of improving an existing design (a bicycle or a salesman's incentive plan) or of finding some way of carrying out a specified activity (circulating air in a building). In the latter case there is a starting point in the various existing ways this is done. The endpoint is again fairly well defined. It may be the successful carrying out of a function, or the practical carrying out of a function, or a cost saving in carrying out a function, or esthetic appeal.

● In innovation the starting point is wide open. The endpoint is also wide open and it is defined in such general terms as success, effectiveness, share of the market. The endpoint can be narrowed. For instance, it may be a matter of innovating a new product which would use existing production facilities, or innovating a new promotion plan which could be dovetailed with the old one.

In general as one moves from problem solving to innovation the definition of starting point and endpoint get vaguer.

In all cases there is a "difficulty gap"; that is to say, one has to pause and change things around before one can proceed further. It is this changing things around that is

166

described as the problem solving, design, or innovating process. This difficulty gap can occur for several reasons:
1. Lack of data.
2. Lack of techniques for handling the data.
3. Lack of ideas for organizing the data into information.
4. Being trapped by old ideas which block the efficient use of available data.
5. Lack of a starting point.

This book is not intended to consider in detail the processes involved in problem solving, design, and innovation. Each process could take a book in itself. The purpose of this section is to show the place of lateral thinking in these processes. This discussion will be followed by a consideration of lateral thinking as it applies to the basic creative process involved in each process.

Problem solving

● Problem solvers often complain that they have worked out ideal solutions but that no one will use them. They complain that they have solved the problem brilliantly but that the person who has to carry through the solution refuses to do so. If this is the case, they have not solved the problem at all. Isolated problems are not real problems. Real problems include not only the specified problem situation but also the "person situation" which includes the people who have to accept and act on the solution. It may be better to have a suboptimal solution which everyone will accept rather than an optimal solution which no one will accept. Lateral thinking can help sell a solution. It is pointless to suppose that if a solution is correct then there is no need to sell it—that its truth will shine for all to see. No one is obliged to accept anything he disagrees with. By a process of lateral change, which involves stating facts in a different way, it is usually possible to present an effective solution in such a way that it makes sense to those who must act on it.

This process of including the "person situation" in the problem context is shown in Figure 14-1.

● Heavy emphasis is usually placed on the importance of problem definition. It is said that once you can define a problem accurately it becomes easy to solve. This is of course true, but it gives the mistaken impression that the

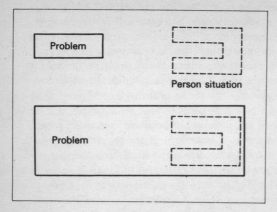

Figure 14–1.

problem definition is a relatively easy matter of language, and the like, and that it takes place as soon as one is presented with the problem. It is supposed that after the definition of the problem there is a period of working things out and then the solution.

In fact, problem definition is very difficult. And, far from being at the beginning of the process, it is toward the end. Once one really has an accurate definition of the problem, he is very close to the solution. The difference between these two attitudes to problem definition is shown in Figure 14–2.

● Problem solving involves a change of state from the beginning state to the end state. The solution provides a channel for this change of state. The appropriateness of this channel depends very much on how the initial state is seen. How is the situation viewed? What factors are

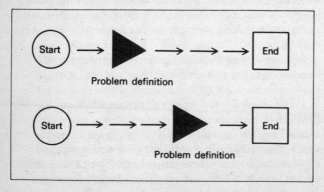

Figure 14–2.

168

considered relevant? What are the features of the situation (for example, wages, workers' satisfaction, union authority, government intervention, productivity, effect on future wage claims, effect on other workers, effect on profits)? The way the situation is parceled into those features is a matter of perceptual choice. Previous sections have dealt with the arbitrariness of perceptual choice, and how it appears to be unchangeable and yet is an arbitrary arrangement of information arising from a personal pattern of experience. Lateral thinking is involved in trying to alter this perceptual choice, in trying to generate alternative ways of looking at the situation; not only when the initial approach is inadequate but also when it appears adequate. For instance, a promotion problem might be looked at in terms of a search for more money, for status, for status for your wife, for a finite measure of success, or as a way to avoid the embarrassment of being unpromoted. But it might also be a simple desire for change of any sort. It might also be a matter of escaping from a particularly awkward personality clash. By looking at the problem in such different ways one may come up with a more effective solution. But the situation by itself will not generate all the different ways it could be looked at. One has to generate the ideas first in order to be able to recognize them.

● Sometimes problems are actually created by particular ways of looking at things. For instance, if you look at bad health as an insurable risk, you are going to have problems which you might not have if you regarded medical care as a service/maintenance contract. Similarly, if you look at the rival gas station on the other side of the motorway as competitive, you would have problems which you would not have if you looked at it as additive to your business.

● The simplest form of difficulty in problem solving is when you set out to solve a problem which is not the one you want to solve. "What plane do I catch to get from city A to city B?" is just another way of saying, "How do I get from city A to city B?" which is just another way of saying "How do I get to see Dr K?" which is another way of saying, "How do I get to see Dr K since he won't come down here?" which is another way of saying, "How do I get to ask Dr K's advice on

this problem?" which is just another way of saying,
"What does Dr K think about this problem?" which is
just another way of saying, "Has Dr K expressed himself
somewhere on this problem?" The answer to the last
statement of the problem may be very different from the
answer to the first statement. The first statement of the
problem would require a timetable (and a lot of time)
for its solution. The last statement would require a call
to a colleague, a librarian, or Dr K himself.

The paradox is that in itself this transformation
process can be very useful and it is the sort of thing one
does with lateral thinking. The value is when one
considers all possible transformations; the danger when
one looks at only one of them.

● FOGWEED is that luxuriant growth of ideas and
elaborations that tends to obscure a problem rather than
clarify it. People who are intensely involved in a problem
are very likely to cultivate fogweed. Fogweed serves no
useful purpose. It exists because it is almost impossible
to stop it growing where the ground is richly fertilized
with information. And once it starts growing it becomes
denser and denser. Elaboration piles upon elaboration
until the basic nature of the problem is lost. Fogweed has
nothing to do with lateral thinking. In fact fogweed is a
vertical thinking process since every branch of thought is
followed vertically as far as possible. Lateral thinking is
concerned with finding different ways of looking at the
basic problem, not with complicating the problem. In
fact, with the PO device lateral thinking provides a sort
of flamethrower to clear away the fogweed. PO implies:
"That may be a very valid way of looking at the
problem; without judging its value, let us try to find
another way."

● Sometimes the sheer availability of a concept (or even of
information) makes it very difficult to solve the problem.
This difficulty is outlined in the section dealing with the
danger of being blocked by openness. There is a natural
feeling that one has to use all the information available.
It is very difficult to realize that a better solution may be
achieved by using only some of the information than by
using it all. For instance, a market research survey may
show that different people like different features in a car.
By trying to design a car to incorporate something for
everybody, one might end up by satisfying no one.

- Three basic types of problem may be distinguished by what is needed for the solution in each case.
  1. Those which can be solved by more information or by better techniques for extracting information from collected data. Such problems are not always as easy to solve as might be suggested because there might be difficulty in deciding *what* new data is required.
  2. Those which can be solved by a rearrangement of already available information. These are the sort of problems which turn out to have an insight solution which tends to be sudden, unexpected, effective, and very elusive. Nor can such solutions be earned by a great deal of effort. It is more a matter of lateral thinking. It is usually a matter of escaping from old ideas which were adequate at one time but which no longer make full use of available information.
  3. That of "no problem". This is the most difficult sort of problem to solve since there is no point at which one can concentrate the problem-solving effort. Where something is being done in a satisfactory way it is difficult to regard it as a possible problem. It is difficult to realize that perhaps one ought to be making a problem-solving effort to find a better way. The only way one might be induced to make this effort is through lateral thinking, which suggests that there is no harm in looking again at things which are taken for granted and appear to be uniquely right. "No problem" is the most important of the three types for it is very rarely tackled, let alone solved. If it were possible to solve it in every case, many of the other types of problem would be solved before they ever arose.

Design

In problem solving the main use of lateral thinking is to find alternative ways of looking at things, to escape from old ideas, and to challenge boundaries and limitations that have been taken for granted. In innovation, the main use of lateral thinking is to get going at all—that is, to generate ideas. The use of lateral thinking in design involves both a need to look at things in different ways and to question assumptions, and a need to get going.

- One may be called on to design a product, a pattern of

organization, or just an idea. The finished design is judged to be satisfactory if it fulfills (or appears to fulfill) certain specifications. These may include such things as simplicity, cost, ease of production, robustness, esthetic appeal, distinctness, in addition to the basic requirement that the product should work. Design usually implies that it is possible to carry out the task set in some way or other, and the design effort is directed to doing it in the best possible way—as defined by the criteria setup. Redesign involves taking an object (or an idea) and altering it so that it carries out its function in a better way.

● With design there is usually a starting point. This may be provided in three ways:
1. A current design which is to be improved.
2. Someone else's design which can be borrowed.
3. An available method for carrying out the desired function even if this method is not incorporated anywhere in a working design.

For instance, in designing a new chocolate confectionery item one might start from a current product, from a competitor's product, or from some way of making chocolate foam.

● Once one has a definite starting point, one has something to work on. One may build on this starting point and carry it further. One may modify this starting point, adding features but also removing other features. One may take the starting point and use it to go in the opposite direction. For instance, in the chocolate confectionery design, one might take an ordinary chocolate bar as the starting point and think in terms of something as unlike a bar as possible—perhaps a coiled tube like a strand of macaroni to give the "thinness" flavor as found in Easter eggs. Once one has a starting point, one can get movement and change, and this is how ideas come about. Instead of spending a long time looking for the most suitable starting point, it is better to get started somewhere and then spend the time moving in all directions from that starting point. It is quite true that there is some danger in being trapped by an inappropriate starting point, but this is unlikely to happen if one uses lateral thinking to move sideways as well as ahead.

● As indicated earlier in this section, the final design has to satisfy a number of requirements. Having found a starting point and having started to move along in one's ideas, how does one keep the design requirements in mind? There seem to be two basic strategies.

1. Move slowly ahead. Be practical at each stage. Examine each step to see if it meets all the requirements. Reject any step which contradicts a requirement.

2. Pursue one or two requirements and ignore all the others. When one has come to a satisfactory design in terms of the chosen requirement, then see how it can be modified to suit all the other requirements as well.

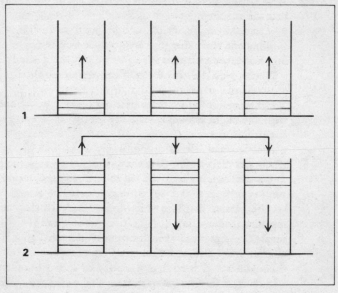

Figure 14–3.

The difference between these two strategies is suggested in Figure 14–3. These two strategies are at opposite ends of a spectrum. In between these extremes are various strategies which deal with a number of the design requirements but not all of them.

The advantage of the second strategy is that it is much easier to keep moving. Because one is satisfying only a single design requirement, he can move ahead. When one finally comes to a satisfactory design in terms of the chosen requirement, he has something to work on in terms of modification, and so on. In effect, by using this method, one is changing an open-ended design situation into a redesign situation—and this is much easier to handle.

In practice one could choose any of the design requirements to pursue before coming back to consider the others. It is more usual, however, to have some sort of hierarchy of importance in the requirements. This is not necessarily based on the actual importance of the requirements. For instance, in real terms such factors as cost and ease of production are obviously of the first importance since failure to meet these requirements would throw out any design. Yet one would prefer to follow a requirement such as simplicity or distinctness of style and, having reached a design based on such a requirement, then come back and look at it in terms of cost and ease of production.

The simplest way of selecting the design requirement to pursue is to consider:

1. The major defect of an existing design.
2. The major advantage the new design is to have over current ones.

These considerations do not apply where a design is totally new and in this case the prime requirement is "apparent usefulness". It is not enough to consider real usefulness because this has little market value at first. More important is the degree of usefulness which is apparent to the *buyer*. It is quite obvious that the purpose of a manufactured object is not simply to work effectively but also to be sold.

The other design strategy is to try to keep all the requirements in mind at each stage. This is much more difficult. If, however, the requirements are additive then it becomes easier. For instance, if one were asked to design a small shopper's car for use in the city, he might have requirements such as: small size, maneuverability, robustness, low pollution factor, ease of access to car and also to storage space, ease of parking, low cost. One could take a lot of these factors into consideration and work within a sort of "envelope" which included such things as electric motors, plastic frames, castor wheels. Another way of carrying out the "all requirements at each stage" strategy is to satisfy each requirement in a particular way and add these results to see what one has.

For instance, in designing an executive training plan, one might list the requirements as short, effective, easily assimilated, theory, case study, project work, field work, assessment. Such a design could be treated in an additive way, as could the design of a bicycle which was to be light, strong, portable, and easy to ride. Additive designs do not exclude compromise between two opposing requirements (such as strength and lightness in the bicycle). In additive designs there is a way of tackling each requirement (use aluminum for lightness, use extra bracing for strength).

But in designing a discount system for major stockists it would not be easy to use the additive strategy. Here the design requirements are that the retailer should continue to buy and sell the product, that he should actively promote the product and not use it as a leader to sell other products, that he should not be in a position to undercut the direct sales force. One might start off by trying to give the retailer as much incentive as possible— for instance, by a volume discount in the standard way. One might then try to improve this by a growth discount which would mean that, if the retailer's turnover increased, an additional discount would be given in proportion to the change in turnover. But this might put the retailer in a position to always undercut the direct sales force—so the original volume discount would be cut. One could in fact adjust the discount so that it was maximal when increase in sales through the retailer equaled sales through the direct sales force.

● Pure functions do not exist. Functions are always wrapped up in a particular way of carrying them out. You can have a glass, a cup, a drinking straw, or a fountain, but not a pure drinking function. In the design process one can try to isolate the pure function and then see how it could be carried out in a new way. Or one could take the standard cliché application and see what could be *trimmed* away.

One might try to define the pure drinking function as "a process which is made possible by the presence of a drinkable liquid in the mouth". One would then think of all the possible ways of getting it there. But even this simple definition already tends to exclude certain ideas by suggesting that the drinkable substance ought to be a fluid. To escape this, one might take as an intermediate impossible: "PO one could drink solids." From this one might go straight to the idea of having the drinkable liquid present as a solid. For instance, by microencapsulation methods the liquid might be contained in tiny capsules pressed together. The whole thing would form an apparent solid which could be cut and handled like a solid. The liquid would then be released by chewing or biting. The general effect would be that of an orange segment.

One might reach this same point by taking a standard application like a drinking cup and try modifying it. A line of thought might go as follows: "A cup is necessary to carry the liquid to the mouth, to prevent it spilling about. Does one need such a strong container? Perhaps a very thin plastic bag would contain the liquid. But how would one handle this? How would one hold it open in order to drink from it? Why not put the whole bag into the mouth instead of trying to drink from it? Different people take different size sips—how big should the bag be? Have a very small bag. Have lots of very small bags and choose the number you want. Perhaps press the small bags together to give a sort of solid. Perhaps use microencapsulation for this." On the whole it is much easier to take a standard idea and work upon it than to try to work from abstractions.

● Starting with a standard design, one can try to trim the surplus features, or split the design into different functions, or extract the really significant function. These are all different degrees of the same process: extraction of the function being one extreme and a little trimming the other extreme.

● When one is using function as the pathway along which to carry the design he might try to find as many ways as possible of carrying out the same function. For instance, one might list cups, drinking fountains, fruit, or ice as different ways of transporting fluid to the mouth. Alternatively, one might take a standard design like a cup to see how many different functions it serves: transport, containment, easy to drink from, stable when put down, decorative, protects hand from heat of liquid. There is nothing magic about the idea of "function". Function is simply a particular way of looking at a design. It happens to be useful. But it can also be limiting if one assumes that in a new design one has to reproduce all the functions that could be discovered in the old design. Functions may easily be there by accident. And even if they are there by design they may still be superfluous.

● The main thing in design is to get somewhere and then start looking backward to satisfy the requirements. And in order to get there one kicks away from the old idea and uses new ideas as stimulants even if they are not directly useful.

Innovation

Innovation differs from problem solving and design in that innovation has no definite starting point. With a problem, the starting point is given by the problem situation. With design, the starting point is given by the old design or by a well-defined function that is to be carried out. The end process, however, is the same in all three processes— satisfaction. One way to set about innovation is to convert it into a problem-solving or design process.

● One can try to find a starting point by creating a problem which does not yet exist. This is done by looking at a situation and picking out the gaps or faults. It is not a matter of finding things that are done wrongly, but of finding things that are not done. For instance, someone might look at the cigarette market and decide that it was a problem that, once started, cigarettes had to be smoked to the end or wasted. From that approach could come the idea of a pack of cigarettes of variable length, or a cigarette which could be pulled apart into various lengths, or a device for neatly extinguishing cigarettes, or a tiny guillotine to cut off the burning end. Another person might decide that the uniformity of taste in a cigarette was a disadvantage and so might come to the idea of a holder which allowed one to add different flavors to whatever cigarette he was smoking. Another person might decide that the problem was to know when to discard a cigarette since the last few puffs were by far the most harmful (being full of condensate from the rest of the cigarette). An easy solution would be to have a black band around this part of the cigarette.

Someone else might look at the ready-to-wear clothes market, and decide that there was a problem in that the customers did not have the same involvement in their clothes which they would have if they made them themselves. This might lead on to the idea of selling clothes in neutral cloth and then allowing the customer to choose from a large selection of easy-to-use dyes. In this way, he would get involvement and also more individuality.

Deliberately creating a problem is a good way to get a starting point for innovation.

● Another method is to take things as they are done and to generate a starting point by using such processes as

1. Combination
2. Separation
3. Transfer

Combination involves taking separate things and putting them together, either in a simple additive way or in a dovetailing way. Adding a dog-walking service to a baby-sitting service is a simple addition. Putting the windscreen-washer jets halfway along the wiper blades is more of a dovetailing, since the usual position does not provide an efficient spray for the wipers to use.

Separation means taking something that carries out a complicated function and breaking it down into separate functions, each of which can be carried out in a better way on its own. For instance, one might separate the decorative function of a dinner plate from its container function by having thin transparent plastic moldings which fitted snugly onto plates which would never be damaged and would never have to be washed. One might separate the long-distance function of a car from its city use by designing special city cars which might be kept (or hired) at peripheral car parks. One might also separate the barrier function of a door from its weather-protection function, and so produce efficient air-curtain systems to keep the temperature up or down and yet leave the door open.

Transfer means taking something from one setting and putting it in another. An innovation can easily result. Often, the transfer is as simple as taking something from one country and introducing it to another where it develops as an innovation because of the different setting. Light Scotch whiskies were not especially popular in England but proved very popular in the United States, so much so that they began to become popular in England. A laboratory device for illustrating the principle of inertia became a best-selling item when transferred to the toy market. Transfer, however, usually involves taking a function that is carried out in a certain way and transferring it to a new field. Shampoos are often packaged in small plastic packets. One could perhaps transfer this form of packaging to hard liquors. Airliners have stewardesses who look after the passengers; why not have stewardesses on trains or at least in certain carriages? Trains have restaurant cars. Perhaps one could have special dinner planes for short flights, with the seats arranged around tables and with food of high quality. Fish have scales to combine strength of material with flexibility; perhaps the idea could be transferred to motor vehicle tires. You can put an immersion heater into a volume of liquid in order to heat it up; what about a cooling probe to cool liquids? Sometimes the transfer can prove useful in a direct way. At other times it may just serve to open up a line of thought. As with other methods, the purpose of a transfer is to provide a *starting point*. Innovation does not consist in the idea itself but the use of that idea in a new setting.

Another way of providing a starting point for innovation is to bring about a distortion. This is rather like setting up an intermediate impossible and seeing what happens. For instance one might say: "PO people had three eyes." This might lead on to such ideas as the redesign of spectacles, detachable eyes in the form of miniature TV cameras, the possibility of training different eyes to do different things, an extra headlight on automobiles, the color of its light varying directly with the speed of the car, the use of trisymmetry in design instead of the usual bisymmetry, stereoscopic TV using a split screen technique, third eye as a signaling device—perhaps a simple flashing-light signaling device with frequency related to emotional strain (at least three settings: tranquil, dynamic, frenzied).

Another distortion might be: "PO people had tiny stomachs." This might lead to such ideas as food preparations which required cooking only once but which remained appetizing as they were eaten in small portions at a time, miniature breeds of cow, pig, and so on, bulking devices for taking a small portion of food and foaming it up into a large amount of eating activity.

The object of the distortion is to introduce new requirements. These new requirements provide a starting point for ideas which can prove useful in themselves quite apart from the distortion. For instance, a food bulking machine would be of interest to any weight watcher.

General points

Certain points which apply to the basic process underlie problem solving, design, and innovation. It is more convenient to deal with these points here than under the separate headings. The points reflect the general principles of lateral thinking.

● *Assumptions, boundaries, limits, specifications.* Problem solving, design, and innovation can be judged as successful only if they satisfy the requirements of the situation. To reach this point one has to make use of certain assumptions. Nevertheless one of the most effective methods for achieving results is to challenge the absolute validity of assumptions, boundaries, limits, and specifications. Once an attitude of challenge rather than acceptance has been set, direct attention to these restrictions will show that they are not unchangeable. And in changing them, one escapes to create a new idea.

● *Simplification.* Any idea which has evolved slowly over a period of time can be simplified. Like a house that is continually added to, such an idea gets bigger and bigger but, as long as it is adequate, no attempt is made to restructure it and to put things together in a more simple manner. Each new addition to the idea is judged to see if it will work, but it is rare for the total idea as a whole to be reexamined. But by such reexamination one can often find shortcuts which simplify the idea without altering its effectiveness. While an idea is evolving, it is difficult to pick out the significant features, so everything is left in (rather like the composite herbal brews in old-fashioned medicine). But with further information one can pick out the essential bits and discard the rest.

● *Cliché units.* Information and ideas are never handled in a pure fashion but only when packaged as some particular pattern. When such patterns prove useful they acquire a life of their own as cliché units. Certain standard ways of carrying out particular functions are examples. One has no choice but to use cliché units, but having used them one can then examine them to see what it is that one really wants from them. A good example of a cliché unit is the old design of automobile directional signals. To imitate a hand stuck out of the window, a movable arm was attached to the side of the car.

● *Leapfrogging.* If one tries to develop an idea steadily, he may come to a point where he is blocked and can go no further. This often happens when a sequential, "vertical thinking", attitude is applied to the creative situation. One needs to be able to leapfrog over these areas of difficulty because, once one has got beyond them, he may find that they are not essential or that it is then easy to find a way round them. Leapfrogging involves treating the area of difficulty as an assumption; for instance, "I don't at the moment know what engine we can use but let us assume that we can find an engine that is cheap and reliable." One then leapfrogs over this area of ambiguity and comes back later on to fill it in as a separate problem in itself. Another advantage of this is that, if the general idea proves unsound, one need not even bother to fill in the leapfrogged gap If, on the other hand, one had had to work steadily through all the difficulties and the general nature of the idea proved unsuitable, there would be a great waste of effort.

● *Get started and move.* Creativity works best when there is something to work on. In problem solving, design, and innovation it is important to find some starting point and then to move forward. Once one is moving and generating ideas, he can always come back, modify the ideas, generate opposite ideas, and so on. This is far better than sitting around and waiting for the perfect idea to arise as a sort of divine inspiration. It is important, however, not to get trapped by a particular starting point or line of thought.

● *Solution image.* It is much easier to work toward a solution image than to just push ahead wondering what will happen next. Also, if there is a solution image it becomes possible to work backward from it. A solution image is some idea of how the problem will be solved, the nature of the successful design, the type of innovation required. Although a solution image makes things much easier, it can also exclude the really new idea. This is because the solution image is inevitably based on the current view of the problem, so a really new idea that falls outside this current view is unobtainable. The more specific the solution image the bigger is this danger. For instance, the solution image to a special city car might take the form: "What we need is a small two-seater car, powered by electricity, and capable of turning in its own length." A more general solution image would be: "Some method of personal transport which would use up the least amount of travel space and provide the maximum convenience."

● *Difficulties created by a way of looking at things.* A particular way of looking at things can create problems or make them difficult to solve (for instance, the idea that workers on strike are just troublemakers). Similarly, a particular way of looking at things may make a design unnecessarily cumbersome and may restrict the area for innovation. One certainly needs points of view in order to start thinking, but one must be aware of the arbitrary nature of a way of looking at things.

● *Beyond the adequate.* It is very easy to stop at the adequate solution to a problem, at the adequate design, at the adequate innovation. Our training and our thinking tools (the functional word NO) provide no incentive for going beyond the adequate. The difference between a good idea and a brilliant idea is often no more than that the brilliant thinker has been dissatisfied with the good idea and spent a little time going beyond it. After all, if you are satisfied then you spend no time at all going beyond this satisfaction point. Dissatisfaction may arise because the thinker is working to some other specification, or because he has some feel for such undefinable things as harmony, economy of effort, elegance, or simplicity. As soon as one realizes that the adequate is not the unique and final answer but only one way of doing things, then one has more incentive to regard it as a starting point rather than as a final objective. If there is time to go further, adequacy should never stop the creative effort.

● *Selection and rejection of ideas.* At the end of the process one has a solution to the problem, a new design, or an innovation. One then has to accept these, put them on one side, or throw them out. There is a natural tendency to simplify the selection task by looking at the idea to find some feature which will allow it to be thrown out before it has to be examined in detail or (worse) actually tried out. This is a very practical attitude. But it has its dangers. There may be a perfectly valid point of rejection in the idea, but it may be possible to keep the idea and get rid of this point of rejection. Even if an idea is to be thrown out, one can look at it to see what is useful in it (in terms of setting off other ideas) instead of just looking at what is wrong in it.

● *Data and ideas.* Data does not by itself generate ideas. It usually does not even suggest them. Data very rarely suggests a way of looking at the data. All it does is amplify or confirm a particular way of looking at it. That is why a different person may find a completely different way of looking at the same data. Data is not information until it has been processed into an idea. It is useless to believe that creative effort can be replaced by a careful accumulation of data. If ideas are needed, more data is no substitute.

● *Information and creativity.* How much information does a creative person need? This is a very practical problem but a difficult one. At one end of the scale, there has to be a certain amount of information (that is to say, data processed into ideas) and experience in order to provide the building blocks for further thought. At the other end of the scale, is the person who is so full of information and experience that he is quite unable to escape from the old ideas in order to generate new ones. As soon as a new idea comes to his mind, such a person will be able to think of reasons why it should not work or how it has been tried out before and failed. Such a person would be quite unable to hold the sort of intermediate impossible that is so necessary for creativity (unless he had been trained in lateral thinking). A rough idea of the relationship between creative effectiveness and information is shown in Figure 14–4. At one end an increase in information causes a greater increase in creativity. But a peak is reached. Beyond that peak more information inhibits creativity. It is not data itself that inhibits creativity but the availability of ideas. The more ideas there are the easier it is to be blocked by openness (as described in a previous section).

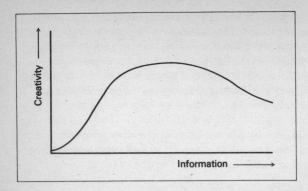

Figure 14-4.

● *What has been left out.* Creativity is not a matter of whether a particular idea is right or wrong. Creativity is not a matter of finding the best way of putting certain things together. Creativity is a matter of trying to get at what has been left out of the original way of looking at the situation. One can never get at this simply by judging the effectiveness of a particular way of looking at the situation. At best, the rejection of a particular idea is no more than a mild invita-

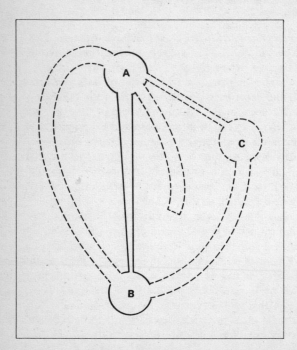

Figure 14-5.

tion to try again. On the other hand an acceptance effectively blocks further search effort. Creativity requires lateral thinking to go beyond the limitations of the YES/NO system in order to get at what has been left out. As suggested in Figure 14–5, it is not a matter of the correctness of the path between A and B but of considering the other paths—and finding them first.

● *Basic processes.* The basic lateral thinking processes involved in problem solving, design, and innovation might be summarized as follows:

ESCAPE from clichés and fixed patterns.
CHALLENGE assumptions.
GENERATE alternatives.
JUMP to new ideas and then see what happens.
FIND new entry points from which to move forward.

Who needs lateral thinking?

15

The answer to this question is the same as the answer to the question: Who needs creativity? Not all creativity stems from lateral thinking, since a creative result can come about through chance stimulation or through an unusual coming together of information. Nevertheless, lateral thinking is the type of thinking that gives rise to creativity.

There was a time when creativity was regarded as being the business of R&D, advertising and marketing, and (perhaps) planning departments. For most organizations, that attitude has passed. Creativity is now recognized as being essential to every sphere of business activity. Attention is now being paid to creativity in such departments as:

Organization and methods
Operational research
Accounting and financial management
Computers and data systems
Management systems
Personnel
Production engineering.

Decision making and selection

The main management function is usually taken to be decision making and the selection of a course of action. This sort of activity does not seem to require creativity for, whereas creativity is open-ended, decision making is (by definition) closed-ended. And yet creativity is an essential part of the process. Creativity comes into the process at three points:

1. In the setting of goals and objectives.
2. In the generation of alternative courses of action from which to select the most appropriate action.
3. In the use of data.

When one looks at the decision-making process, it is easy to suppose that both objectives and possible courses of action are neatly set out and that the available data has only to be looked at for it to provide a reason for selecting a particular course of action. This sort of artificial situation applies more often in management books than in real life. In real life, one has to work creatively in order to set up objectives, to explore the alternative courses of action, and to look at the data in such a way that it yields the maximum of information. It *is* possible to proceed by accepting a routine objective, being satisfied with the obvious course of action, and finding in the data only what one expects to find. But this is not a very satisfactory way of proceeding.

Standardized management training

Today more than ever there is a danger in the very excellence of available management techniques and training. As soon as something has proved its worth, it is adopted by managements everywhere. The advantage of superior techniques is obvious, and one would hardly want to revert to the haphazard seat-of-the-pants approach of hunch management. On the other hand, the sheer uniformity of management techniques and attitudes puts creativity at an even higher value than before. Without creativity, everyone will find himself looking at the situation in the same way and reacting in the same way. The competitive advantage will go to the person who is capable of supplementing the available management techniques with enough creativity to be able to see the situation in a unique way. As in so many other fields, the growth of effectiveness, far from diminishing the need for creativity, actually increases that need.

Management levels and creativity

In large organizations, creativity is often handed over as an area of interest to those who need it least. Anyone who is working in an R&D department already has some creativity and probably some skill in its use. It is not here that creativity is most needed. It is the ordinary line managers who have more need of it, for these are the people who do not habitually practice creativity and who may have found that they can get by without it. The whiz-kids in an organization are often whiz-kids because they manage to combine effectiveness with creativity. But for everyone else a rise up the promotional ladder is usually the reward for qualities quite other than creativity. The higher the position a person

holds the more he needs creativity, since he becomes involved
in overview and policy situations instead of routine line
management functions. And yet the person who reaches this
position has often done so because he has exhibited those
necessary qualities of drive and efficiency rather than any
special skill in creativity, for at the lower management levels
the opportunities to show creativity are few. It is for this
reason that some skill in lateral thinking is even more
necessary to those whose normal activities do not appear to
require creativity than it is for those who are in a more
obviously creative situation. Lateral thinking is a skill that
can be developed and not just a gift for which one ought to
be grateful.

Mistaken notions

Three common notions deter people from trying to develop
skill in creativity.
1. "That ideas will come about of their own accord when the
   time is ripe."
   It is quite true that ideas do come about of their own
   accord. At least, one notices those that do come about but
   cannot notice the non-occurrence of those which do not
   come about. Unfortunately, the ideas may come about in
   the mind of someone else and, even if this is not directly
   inconvenient, it means that one does not have the advantage
   of being *ahead* with the idea. When ideas do come about
   of their own accord, they usually do so long after they
   could have come about (in terms of available information).
   When ideas come about only through the pressure of
   events it may often be too late to make use of them.
   With creativity one tries to bring ideas about as soon as
   they become possible—rather than wait until they are
   inevitable.
2. "That if one has formal techniques for handling information one does not need creativity."
   This is an unfortunate misconception. There is no clash
   between creativity and formal techniques. Lateral thinking
   is concerned with the first stage of thinking that decides
   how the situation is looked at. After this has been done,
   one then moves ahead with the formal techniques such as
   mathematics, statistics, linear programming. The misconception is particularly unfortunate because where there
   is an available formal technique some attention to the

first stage of thinking can enhance the effectiveness of that technique. Yet no amount of excellence in the application of the techniques can make up for a wrong approach to the problem.

3. "That lateral thinking may serve only to confuse and diminish the efficiency of vertical thinking."

This notion is more often felt than stated. Some people do get upset by the different use of information in lateral thinking, and they fear that if they get used to thinking in this way then they will be unable to use the full vigor of vertical thinking when this is required. This attitude shows a basic misunderstanding of lateral thinking, which is concerned only with changing or generating ideas and not with their processing.

Twin aspects of lateral thinking

The first aspect of lateral thinking is the generation of new ideas. The second aspect is the escape from old ones. Even if one does not wish to go so far as to add the generative power of creativity to his thinking, it is still very useful to be able to escape from old ideas. Whether one is called on to create new ideas or not, the possibility of escaping from old ideas is there all the time. In effect, when one does escape from an old idea, he comes up with a new idea, but this is not the same as sitting down with the intention of generating a new one. Generating new ideas requires more skill in lateral thinking than escaping from old ones. Even if one does not actually succeed in escaping from the old idea, some knowledge of lateral thinking will lessen the arrogance with which the idea is held. This means that the idea becomes easier to change should circumstances alter (new information, someone else's point of view, et cetera).

Applications of lateral thinking

In practice lateral thinking will tend to be used on the following occasions. These are not the only occasions on which it would be used nor are these occasions mutually exclusive.

1. Direct innovation such as with a new product, a new marketing idea, a new organizational idea.
2. Simplification of an idea that has evolved gradually and become rather cumbersome. Such simplification may

involve a shortcut, a restructuring, or a redesign. Value engineering is a good example of this process.

3. Periodic reassessment of ideas that seem quite adequate, in the hope of finding better ways of doing things. This may involve a switch to a new idea or a simplification of the existing idea (as in 2).
4. Problem solving.
5. Taking advantage of a change in circumstances or new information.
6. Looking at data in different ways in order to extract the maximum amount of information from it.
7. Creative response. This involves the response to a plan, policy, or idea put forward by someone else.
8. Prevention of sharp divisions, polarizations, and rigid concepts.

The cost of creativity

Many people feel that creativity is an expensive luxury since the development of new ideas is very expensive (retooling, production changes, market research, promotion, and the like) and the large majority of new product ideas fail (seven out of every ten). Such people feel that it is better to wait until someone else has developed the idea and opened up the market, and then to follow behind as quickly as possible. The disadvantages and advantages of such a policy aside, it is possible to point out that the innovation of new products is but one aspect of creativity. On the whole, lack of creativity is more costly than creativity. Lack of creativity means continuing to do things in an inefficient way long after they could have been altered. Lack of creativity means pursuing the same concepts after they have gone out of date. Lack of creativity means becoming committed to a cumbersome data retrieval system because it follows directly from the system currently in use. Lack of creativity means raising capital in an expensive way because that is the way it has always been done.

Problem solving

Problems are change points. Most change situations which require any thought can be looked at as problems. It may be a matter of being faced with a specific problem, identifying a problem, or even creating a problem. Problem solving is not

190

confined to any one segment of management, though the nature of the problem obviously varies from department to department. Lateral thinking is used in problem solving in three ways:
1. Before any attempt is made to tackle the problem at all. Lateral thinking is used to generate different approaches.
2. When a problem proves impossible to solve with ordinary vertical thinking methods.
3. When an apparently adequate solution has been reached but one wants to go beyond this to find other solutions.

Routine part of thinking

Though there are specific occasions when lateral thinking tends to be used it should, nevertheless, be regarded as a *routine* part of thinking. Anyone who thinks needs to understand lateral thinking—and might benefit by developing some skill in it. Creativity is everybody's business.

The management of creativity

The management of creativity could be regarded as the management of creative results. This would involve such things as the development and marketing of new ideas after they have come about. The new ideas themselves may have originated within an organization or may have been borrowed from another organization. This type of activity might be regarded as venture management. This book is more concerned, however, with the generation of new ideas rather than the handling of them once they have come about. The handling of new ideas may be a creative exercise in itself but it depends heavily on the skillful application of sound management techniques. It is the generation of new ideas that really demands the creativity, and this book is concerned with this part of the process. That is why the term lateral thinking has been preferred to creativity because creativity is the description of a result which may have come about in several different ways (not all of them creative), whereas lateral thinking refers only to the creating process.

There are two basic aspects of the management of lateral thinking. The first aspect is concerned with lateral thinking as a necessary part of the thinking process. This aspect deals with the development of some skill in lateral thinking in everyone who is required to show creativity. The second aspect is concerned with the organization and use of lateral thinking as a special creative function which may be carried out by specified groups.

General use of lateral thinking

As discussed in previous sections, lateral thinking is concerned with the first stage of thinking—the setting up of concepts and the approach to a situation. It is concerned as much with escaping from old ideas as with generating new ones. And all the time it is concerned with making fuller use of available information. For these reasons lateral thinking is a part of the ordinary thinking process, and is not a luxury tool of use only to those who are required to be creative in a deliberate fashion.

In time, the principles of lateral thinking may come to be incorporated into general education or at least into management education. Until then, it is necessary to develop skill in lateral thinking as a supplement to conventional education.

The first step is awareness of the nature of lateral thinking and its application. Such awareness (and hopeful understanding) is a necessary step toward developing skill in lateral thinking. In any case, an awareness of the process allows one to respond to the use of lateral thinking by others even if he is unable to use it himself. This first step of awareness is effected by getting executives to read through a book such as this. They may find that certain points in the book confirm what they already do. They may find that the book gives them confidence in creative thinking. They may find that certain sections give them more insight and understanding into the creative process. They may decide to practice some of the techniques described.

Even if the process goes no further than this general awareness, it may bring about a considerable change in attitude toward creativity which may come to be regarded as a way of using information and as a learnable skill instead of being treated as a magic gift. From such a first step, awareness may spark an interest in the subject, and this interest can be developed further. It does not matter how big a starting step may be, as long as there is a starting step.

The second step is the use of special training situations or even outside courses to provide some practice in the use of lateral thinking. (Group training methods and personal training methods have already been described in the section on training.)

The important point about the general use of lateral thinking is that everyone should be made aware of the purpose of the process and the principles involved. It is better for everyone to have a somewhat superficial knowledge of the subject than for a few people with a special interest to explore the subject in depth. Since lateral thinking is a totally different way of using information, it is very difficult for those who use lateral thinking to communicate easily with those who have no knowledge at all of it. Thus a superficial knowledge of lateral thinking enables one to make full use of the lateral thinking specialist even if one does not use the process oneself.

As suggested in an earlier section, the actual amount of time or effort spent on lateral thinking is not important. What is important is that some time be spent on it in order to show the need for creative discontinuity and some ways of bringing it about. Five minutes spent on acquiring the lateral thinking attitude is more useful than five hours of trying to be creative.

Special use of lateral thinking

Just as one may use a computer to work out statistics or a legal expert to provide legal services, so one might want to use lateral thinking in a specific way in order to provide creativity. The specific way may involve the use of someone who is specially skilled in lateral thinking, or a group skilled in this function, or a formal setting in which lateral thinking is to be used. This special use of lateral thinking is not an alternative to the general use described above. No amount of special use can substitute for the general use, any more than the availability of computers makes it unnecessary for an executive to think logically. Special use simply involves using a special tool for special occasions, just as one might paint the garden fence oneself but employ an artist to paint a mural on the wall.

Outside groups

Creativity can be obtained from outside. This can be done in several ways:

1. Direct borrowing of ideas developed elsewhere. These may involve new products, new solutions to problems, new techniques. Such borrowing could involve the payment of license fees or even the employment of someone who has developed his special knowledge elsewhere.
2. Direct use of an outside creative agency. Such agencies may exist as new product development groups or as problem-solving think tanks. Contract research organizations can also be used especially when the problem has been narrowed down and defined.
3. Use of a creative organizing agency. Here the agency does not undertake to provide the ideas but comes into the organization and organizes such things as brainstorming sessions among the executives in the organization. The ideas then arise from within the organization under the impetus of outside stimulation.
4. Use of a creative consultant. A creative consultant is specially skilled and experienced in lateral thinking. He does not bring with him any special knowledge concerning the firm's business. What he does bring is an ability to find out how things are being looked at and to suggest new ways of looking at them. The creative consultant serves as a special sort of mirror. He does not provide information but simply reflects what is provided for him. But in reflecting it he changes things around and puts things together in a new way. This process can itself provide a creative solution or at least the starting point for such a solution. In this capacity, the consultant may succeed in putting things together in a new way, or he may succeed only in showing that the problem is being looked at in a particular, fixed manner. Even this is of some help because one becomes more able to escape from a fixed idea if the idea has been identified.

The use of outside creativity has several advantages and disadvantages:

Advantages:
1. A specialist agency can provide a higher degree of creative talent than could be assembled within an average organization (because of selection, training, and sheer bulk of practice).
2. The experience accumulated by a specialist agency will allow it to see the conceptual blocks more easily than others not so experienced.

3. Within an organization information comes in piece by piece over a period of time. The final arrangement of the information into an idea is thus heavily dependent on the time sequence of arrival. An outside agency has the huge advantage that all the information is presented simultaneously and is thus independent of the time sequence of arrival. The advantage of this is discussed on page 32.
4. It is cheaper to hire creativity for a specific purpose (or to borrow or buy ideas) than to set up a whole structure to generate them.
5. Inevitably, an outside agency has a different point of view unless it has been used so often by the same corporation that it has assumed the corporation point of view. In any case, an outside agency is outside the personality structure, which may be inhibiting the development of new ideas within the organization. For instance, an outside agency might simply bounce back an idea originally provided by someone too unpopular or too junior to have his idea accepted.

Disadvantages:
1. By pushing creativity out to an agency, one does nothing about developing creativity within the organization. In fact one may actually feel that there is no need to do anything about it in the circumstances. And yet creativity is a necessary part of thinking, not something required only on special occasions.
2. The outside agency may not be able to make full use of the unique and individual knowledge or marketing opportunities available to a particular organization. An outside agency is more inclined to supply "off the peg" solutions.
3. There is a slight danger of information being unconsciously transferred from one organization to another since the agency deals with a number of clients. This is not very important, especially where agencies do not provide ready-made ideas but work to bring out ideas that are latent within the firm.
4. When an agency does turn up a new idea, it is easy to feel that the idea is so obvious that it would have been thought of anyway without having brought in the agency. This may be true and an agency may take credit for ideas that would have developed naturally—or were even kicking around. On the other hand, it is very easy to say an idea is obvious *once it has come about*.

5. It is easy enough to call in a creative agency when there is a specific problem to be solved or a new product needed, but it is difficult to call in an agency when there is the problem of no problem (see page 171). It is difficult for an outside agency to provide the creativity that is needed as part of ordinary decision making, planning, and reaction to information.
6. Since an outside agency is paid to produce ideas, there may be a tendency to inflate the value of moderate ideas rather than admit failure. The organization may then be blocked by an idea that is only adequate.
7. It is very difficult to judge the effectiveness of an outside agency. One can go by past successes but one success can carry an agency much further than it deserves to go.
8. It may be difficult to judge the proper cost for use of an agency. When creativity takes place within an organization, it is easier to operate in terms of the potential advantage because creativity work can be used to take up the slack of other employment.

The balance between the advantages and disadvantages is an individual one in each case. The decision whether or not to employ an outside agency depends on several factors.

● Urgency and size of the problem to be solved.
● Possibility of its being solved within the organization. Has thinking within the organization come to a dead end?
● Availability of a first-class outside agency.
● Size of organization: is the organization big enough to afford its own creative team? If so, such a team improves with use.
● Quality of creative talent within the organization as based on present assessment and past performance.
● Availability of money for this purpose.

The biggest danger in the use of outside agencies is the accompanying tendency to neglect creativity training within the company. No matter how often an outside agency is used, there is no excuse for neglecting training in lateral thinking within the company. The idea that all the creativity required by a firm can be bought from outside sources is nonsense.

In-house use

The general use of lateral thinking within an organization has been discussed earlier. This section deals with the special use of lateral thinking groups or individuals.

Court jester

In ancient royal courts, the court jester served a particular function. He was there to serve as a butt for jokes. He was also there to be amusing and entertaining (and possibly to laugh at the king's jokes when no one else would). But, in order to be amusing, he had to take an unusual view of things and turn inside out something which would otherwise have been routine and dull. No one expected him to be serious but they did expect him to be witty, and this usually involved looking at something in an unusual but valid way. The court jester did not have to persuade anyone to adopt his point of view, but once a point of view had been offered then it was difficult to hide it again if it made sense. It was precisely because the court jester had no direct responsibility that he could afford to find unusual ways of looking at things. There was even some incentive to find the most way-out ideas because these would increase his value as an entertainer. It is important to remember that the court jester operated at the most senior level possible. He had direct access to the king's ear. There were no intervening officials to filter the outrageousness of the jester's view of things.

The court jester filled a very important lateral thinking role. When faced with a situation, the king was able to see it only in terms of his own limited experience. Nor could he rely on his courtiers to provide an alternative point of view because their opinions were much colored by their ambitions. It was the role of the court jester to restructure things in a lateral way and so provide a different point of view. The king might have liked this new point of view or it might have triggered an inside switch-over to a new point of view. Or the jester's extreme point of view might have modified the king's original view. Or the jester's point of view might have served as an intermediate impossible, or it might have served as a provocative arrangement of information to bring about a self-revealing response from the courtiers. All these are natural lateral thinking functions since the jester was using information not in an analytical or descriptive manner but in a way that resulted in an unpredictable effect.

Ideally, one would like to resurrect the court jester role in the management situation. It would have to operate at the highest managerial level where ultimate plans, policies, and decisions were made. It is at this level that information is presented as the setting for some decision action. It is at this level that different ways of looking at information can be most useful. To have a court jester at a lower level would be quite useless.

Occasionally there is a natural court jester at this level. This person can always be relied on to come up with a different way of looking at things. This is quite a different role from that of the persistent critic who is eternally negative. The court jester comes up with new and stimulating ideas, not just with holes in ideas.

In the absence of a natural court jester, executives could take it in turn to adopt the court jester role just as people find it useful to adopt the role of devil's advocate from time to time. Once the concept of the court jester's role has been appreciated, this use of lateral thinking becomes possible.

de B gland

In the human body the hormone-producing glands are very tiny structures, but they have an effect out of all proportion to their size. Their effect is not a direct one, but they serve to stimulate other processes. A de B gland (for want of a better name) is a small group of people formally set up in order to provide the court jester function. The business of this group of three, four or five people would be to think laterally all the time. Their role would be to suppose that the way things were being done was the silliest way of doing them. They would question adequate ways of doing things and challenge assumptions. Without any executive responsibility, they would come up with wild ideas. No one would be expected to act on the ideas of this group, but they would be expected to *listen* to the ideas.

For the de B gland to function effectively, it would have to have good lines of communication to management at all levels. This would mean that the group should contain someone who could himself communicate at all levels or else it would pass on its views to someone who could communicate them. The other important point is that the de B gland should have no departmental allegiance or executive responsibility. It would be an idea-generating group rather than a problem-solving group.

The people making up the de B gland would stay with it

only a short time—perhaps one month, and then they would move back to their own positions. Ideally, the executive would be freed of his other duties for this period. If this were not possible, he would undertake the de B gland function as well. But this is much less satisfactory. Apart from its usefulness in generating ideas, the de B gland would serve as a short conceptual holiday to the executives as they rotated through it. Freed from the usual inhibitions and restrictions, the executive could spend this holiday generating ideas and practicing lateral thinking. If nothing else, his period in the de B gland would purge him of all the ideas that had been building up in his mind but had never found a suitable outlet. To some, it could even be a safety valve for the stress of modern business.

Think-tank sessions

Think-tank (or brainstorming) sessions could be used to provide a lateral thinking function. Such sessions could be set up with the people involved in the problem or they could involve people outside the problem. A permanent group of skilled lateral thinkers might be set up, and they would be called together either on a regular basis or from time to time in order to think laterally about some problem. Instead of being permanent members of the group, the participants could rotate through it. A better alternative would be for part of the group to be permanent members and for the rest to consist of the people involved in the particular problem.

The nature and function of a brainstorming group have been described in a previous section (see pages 115 to 131).

Timing

It is customary to look for creativity when there is a problem to be solved or a new product to be invented. When this point is reached, then a deliberate effort is made to use lateral thinking either by bringing in an outside agency or by setting up a think-tank session. This process is shown in Figure 15-1. Everything is flowing smoothly. Then comes the problem. The problem is packaged and turned over to the problem solvers. Then things run on smoothly until the next problem. This is rather an inefficient way of using creativity. Once a problem has been set up, the solutions to that problem may be limited. But if creativity had been used at an earlier point, a different line of action may have been chosen and the problem situation may never have arisen. This involves the parallel use of creativity instead of the sequential use. In this parallel process, the creative group keeps an eye on the decision process all the time. The creative group may actually be involved in the process but, if this is inconvenient, it should at least receive frequent reports on what is happening.

The difference between the sequential use of creativity and the parallel use is shown in Figure 15–1.

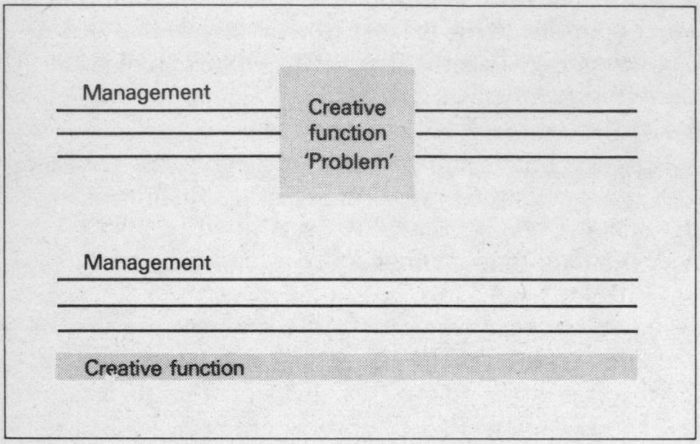

Management

Creative
function
'Problem'

Management

Creative function

Figure 15–1.

Decisions and lateral thinking

It is obvious that creativity is needed in problem solving, design, and innovation. But its place in decision making is not so obvious. After all, decisions can be made without the help of creativity. If there is only one choice, then the decision is easy; if there are more choices, it is still a matter of decision making rather than creativity. If there are no obvious courses of action, then it is called a problem—and creativity may be used. A decision is only a special sort of problem, and the presence of possible courses of action does not eliminate the need for creativity. Creativity may be used in the decision-making process at three points:

1. In the collection of information and, particularly, in generating different ways of looking at this information.
2. In generating different courses for action beyond the obvious courses that suggest themselves.
3. In considering decisions that have already been made and especially the consequences of a decision.

It may be felt that the generation of alternative courses of action would simply be confusing. But who would want to make decisions easier by being deliberately ignorant of possible courses of action? The more possible courses of action there are generated, the more valid is the choice of any one of them.

Organization

The inspirational attitude to lateral thinking is not very helpful. It usually ends up with a few people becoming very interested, to the extent that everyone else feels that it is a specialist matter best left alone. To be effective, lateral thinking needs to be placed within an organization structure. There is a need for formal envelopes in which to practice lateral thinking (defined time, place, people) and a formal framework to relate the lateral thinking to actual problems.

Concept manager

There may in time be established the position of concept manager. Just as there are at present financial managers, research managers, organization managers, so there will be concept managers. The role of the concept manager will be to control and generate the "concept capital" of the organization. This will include creativity, new ideas, adaptation to change, definition of objectives.

In practice the concept manager will collect ideas and idea people. He will provide training and set up channels of communication. Creativity will be one of his special functions. This function will be removed from the R&D department, where it does not properly belong since creativity is much wider than the invention of new products.

Until such time as concept managers are appointed, the organization of lateral thinking may fall into the hands of the training officer, the OR department, the planning department, or R&D. The actual label is not so important. What is important is avoiding the impression that lateral thinking is the special *preserve* of any one department.

Framework

The framework involves the organization of training sessions, courses, brainstorming sessions, distribution of literature, and so on. There is the matter of deciding what form training should take, who should be involved, how often sessions should be held, and for how long. In all this there are two important considerations to keep in mind:

1. Not to overdo things, especially as regards frequency and duration of sessions. One hour every two weeks would be ample.
2. To be sure to set up some definite framework and not rely on interest or inspiration.

Communication

The lines of communication of any lateral thinking group are most important. It is quite useless to have a bright group generating ideas in a vacuum. This could happen because no one will call them in to look at real problems, or because their ideas have no way of reaching the decision makers.

The business of exploiting new ideas is every bit as important as generating them. Quite apart from special lateral thinking groups, one ought to set up channels of communication to encourage the flow of ideas and suggestions, for once encouraged these start to flow. Whether the people generating these ideas are consciously using lateral thinking or not hardly matters.

It is obviously impractical to act on every idea, yet some sort of recognition that the idea has been looked at is necessary. Otherwise, people get discouraged and dry up. It is not just a matter of recognizing the great new idea but of acknowledging the humble idea.

Control and freedom

Control seems to be the opposite of freedom and yet it is difficult to enjoy freedom without control. It is difficult to exercise free lateral thinking unless there is some formal structure available. The balance between control and freedom is delicate. One large organization used to circulate a sheet asking for way-out ideas on a certain problem. Each worker was supposed to contribute his idea and sign the sheet. To the surprise of the management the ideas never seemed very creative. Because lateral thinking is a formal and deliberate procedure there is the tendency to try to control every aspect of it just as one might control a stock inventory. The other extreme is to do nothing and to suppose that left alone in total freedom people will come up with great ideas. They do not.

What one does is to set up formal envelopes and then let people play around freely within these envelopes and, at the end, collect and channel the creative efforts. It is not a matter of running control and creativity in parallel, because this is impossible, but of alternating them as suggested in the diagram in Figure 15 2. Too much structure is as sterile as too little structure.

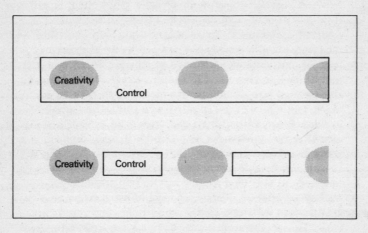

Figure 15–2.

Personnel

The three usual aspects are:

1. SELECTION
2. TRAINING
3. EMPLOYMENT

Selection. This may involve the use of various creativity tests but the best test remains performance. Where possible one would prefer to employ people on a trial basis in order to watch their creativity in action. A past record is almost as valid.

Training. This includes the general training in lateral thinking for everyone and also the special training for those who are going to be employed in a more intensely creative capacity. The three basic points of training are:

203

1. Understanding the process
2. Practice
3. Confidence

Training methods are discussed in the section on training on page 158.

Employment. This refers to the use of exploitation of creative people. Whether the creative temperament really exists or not, it is well to be aware of it and while making allowance for it to avoid being bullied by it.

When creative people are involved, a group situation differs from one without creative people. Instead of the group being a sort of committee to arrive at a neutral compromise idea, the creative group is arranged as a setting for the development of individual ideas. Instead of individual identity being pushed back to give a sort of group average, the individual is allowed to leap ahead with his ideas and to pull the group along with him. The group provides a soil for the growth of his idea. Whereas soundness and breadth of view is the aim of most group discussions with creative people, stimulation is the only purpose of a group.

Many creative people seem ineffective when working on their own. It may be difficult to try to improve their effectiveness by exhortation. Ideally, one would like to team up a creative man with an executor who would carry through the ideas. This combination would be much more powerful than the creative man on his own. Another useful combination is to put the creative man together with an information man. This is someone who has developed the "library attitude". This means that he is so stocked with information on the subject that he is quite incapable of developing ideas of his own. The creative man uses the information to move ahead and create new ideas.

Only too often, a creative man who is not interested in administration is promoted into an administrative position. This follows from the usual salary promotion structure. The result is that a good creative man is lost and a poor administrator gained. It is not too difficult to alter the promotion structure to allow sideway promotion with an increase in salary and status but no change in work.

For creative people, salary is not as important an incentive as freedom, opportunity, and facilities. It is clear that an organization would be unable to support all its research workers while they worked on any project which pleased them and ignored the product demands of the company. On the other hand, there is no harm in offering the workers a portion of their time for work on their own projects. Where this has been tried it seems to have had a good effect on motivation. Moreover, the research workers did not take advantage of the private time offered to them—it was enough to know it was available if required. Another type of incentive is to allow research workers to use facilities up to a certain limit without having to go through complicated application procedures. In one situation where workers were allowed to order up to $2000 worth of equipment on their own initiative, it was found that the average order was about one-twentieth of this. Yet the presence of the opportunity acted as an incentive.

Temperament and creativity

A myth has its own reality. Much of the idea of the "creative temperament" is a myth. Much of it is a stereotype. Nevertheless, as a myth or a stereotype, the idea of a creative temperament does exist. This temperament is claimed by creative people for themselves and often recognized in creative people by others. Even if creative temperament has no scientific basis, it would still be necessary to treat it as a reality. If a person chooses to wear a bright yellow baseball cap you do not make the cap disappear by showing that there is no need to wear it.

Instead of trying to prove the necessity for the creative temperament, one acknowledges its existence at least as a myth. Whether it is a myth or real, one may end up by treating it in the same way. This does not much matter. What is very important, however, is to realize that though the creative temperament is to be found in creative people it is not related to the degree of creativity. Moreover, creativity is to be found in people who exhibit none of the manifestations of the creative temperament. This is a very important point. There are creative people who make a big production of the creative temperament which then becomes not an index of their creativity but an amplifier of what creative talent they have. Because the creative temperament is usually quite visible it is too easy to accept it as a valid index of real creativity which is never very visible since it is but the potential for achievement. Only when achievement has come about often enough can one recognize true creativity—but this cannot be done in advance. It is possible to use various psychological tests to show up a tendency which is rather more likely to be associated with creativity than is a lack of that tendency. As with most psychological tests, however, there is the danger that the tests touch only one part of the subject yet invite complete concentration on this measurable part to the exclusion of other less measurable but (conceivably) more important parts of the picture.

The creative ego

Cultures which do not encourage a strong ego structure do not seem to be as creative as those which are more interested in individuals than in groups. Although this ego activity may not be an essential part of creativity, it may serve as a mechanism for encouraging creativity if there is no other mechanism available. One of the purposes of lateral thinking is to make it unnecessary to rely on such mechanisms. There are three reasons why a strong ego structure might encourage creativity:

1. There is need for individual courage or confidence to pursue an eccentric idea. An eccentric idea is simply one which is not at once acceptable by the group. An eccentric idea may be a very valid idea which is just too new to fit into the old patterns and hence cannot be accepted until it is properly linked into these old patterns or has been around long enough to show its usefulness. An eccentric idea may also be an idea which really is ridiculous and the group's judgment is right in this respect. Nevertheless, by pursuing the idea the egotist may come through to a valid idea. In this case the invalid idea serves as an intermediate impossible (as discussed in a previous section). In order to pursue ideas which are not immediately acceptable to the group, one needs courage, confidence, or true madness. Other things which can help toward this effect are actual isolation or virtual isolation when the group shows little direct interest in one's ideas.

   The idea of the intermediate impossible and the use of PO in lateral thinking is to allow the group to accept eccentric ideas as possible stepping-stones to new ideas. This reduces the need for ego strength.

2. A strong ego will find it difficult to accept things simply because they are acceptable. A strong ego often leads to a state of chronic dissatisfaction which involves the

questioning of the way things are done. This sort of personality will be inclined to look beyond the adequate answer to find something better. This sort of personality finds acceptance difficult. This difficulty may be expressed as a creative urge to find something better but it may as easily be expressed as a continual negative criticism.

One of the functions of lateral thinking is to develop the ability to question established ideas and to look beyond the adequate not because of chronic dissatisfaction but through a realization that any particular way of doing things is but one way.

3. A strong ego is very much concerned with its individuality, uniqueness, and identity. This sort of personality will always be looking for ways of standing out, of being different, of gaining attention. This gaining attention is not an essential part of the picture, for a person may be content to know that he is going his own way whether or not anyone else notices this. The desire to stand out from the group is in contrast to the desire to fit into the group and to make life easier by eliminating differences. A byproduct of this need to be different is the generation of new ideas and new ways of looking at things—or at least an interest in these if one is not capable of generating them for oneself.

In all three of the points made above the term "strong ego" does not refer to the usual meaning of strength, for a truly strong ego may be very content to fit in with a group. As used above the term "strong" refers more to a "pronounced" or "marked" ego structure. It is more a need to develop a strong ego than the possession of one.

Motivation

The creative temperament is more interested in the nature of the idea itself than the usefulness of that idea in achieving something else. This leads to a number of tendencies:

1. An idea is often valued for its newness, its originality, or its ingenuity quite apart from its actual worth.
2. It is difficult to arouse interest in boring or routine subjects no matter what incentive is offered.
3. Interest in an idea is sufficient incentive for it to be pursued with great application even in the face of difficulties and at the expense of personal convenience.
4. There is a tendency to start off with an idea and then to

switch to something quite different, leaving behind the half-finished initial idea and being labeled a "butterfly mind". Often this switching about simply results from the continual emergence of new and exciting ideas in the mind of a creative person. It is not so much that he lacks application but that (unlike others) he is overwhelmed by the temptation to pursue new ideas.

5. The creative temperament is more likely than any other to be upset at the frustration of not being able to pursue a line of interest.

6. The creative temperament finds it difficult to be interested in other people's ideas.

The creative temperament may be impractical

It is not that the creative temperament is incapable of being practical but simply that practicality does not have the dominant position which it has in the thinking of non-creative temperaments. The creative temperament may seem to be impractical for several reasons:

1. Interest shifts from the usefulness of an idea to the nature of the idea itself.

2. Inspiration is given a greater importance than information. It is easy to carry this attitude to ridiculous extremes (either way).

3. A creative person may be too excited about seeing what happens next to spend the necessary time on the apparatus for trying out the idea. The unfortunate result is that a very good idea may be lost because it has been tried out in an incompetent manner.

4. In hot pursuit of a developing idea, a creative person may be unable to step back and look at the whole picture (in terms of organization, et cetera).

5. A creative temperament may have such ego involvement in an idea that he is unwilling to give it up when it proves uneconomical.

Acceptance of ideas

1. Though countries with a strong ego bias often appear to be more creative, they also appear to have more difficulty in using ideas. The creative temperament is good at generating ideas but very poor at accepting the ideas of others. And since the use and development of an idea

usually rely on people other than the originator, difficulty in accepting the ideas of others can be a severe disadvantage. In countries which do not have a strong ego bias, an idea is not regarded as a personal thing at all but as an intellectual event which has happened somewhere in the intellectual landscape. Just as a tree in a landscape is there to be looked at by everyone, so an idea is there to be looked at and used by everyone. As a consequence, there is no jealousy and defensiveness when ideas are exploited for what they are worth. This is something a creative temperament finds hard to do.

2. Just as the creative temperament finds it hard to appreciate the ideas of others, so it is difficult to set a creative temperament to work on an idea which comes from another source. One much-used tactic is to pitch the new idea at somewhat below its full value. Then the creative person to whom the idea is put can make his contribution by extending the idea. And once he has made this contribution, he becomes sufficiently involved to work on the idea.

3. A creative temperament has so much ego involvement in an idea that there is much resentment when the idea is rejected or shelved. It is difficult for a creative temperament to realize that the mere newness or brilliance of an idea does not make it useful. Nor has anyone an obligation to adopt an idea just because it is new or is a great creative idea. If the idea does have value, then it is up to the originator of the idea to put this value across to whoever has to act on the idea. No one has any obligation to act on an idea unless he can see the point of it.

Creative temperaments are difficult to work with

The following points apply more to the caricature of the creative temperament than to most creative people. The characteristics are, however, exhibited in some degree by less extreme forms of the temperament.

1. Motivational difficulties (as discussed elsewhere in this section).
2. Inability to accept the ideas of others.
3. A certain arrogance in the divine right of creativity.
4. Inarticulateness and difficulty in communicating.
5. Lack of discipline and rejection of the need to do things that are not directly interesting.

6. Easily aroused impatience and frustration.
7. Difficulty in working in a team situation except as a leader, and leadership qualities are not always present. Difficulty in accepting group dilution of an idea by compromise or modification.
8. Too strong a sense of the idea of creativity.

Polarization

Creativity can become a refuge. On reading about lateral thinking, people are apt to make remarks such as:
"I am a natural lateral thinker."
"I always wondered why I did not get on with vertical thinkers."
"I have always used lateral thinking without realizing it."
There is a tendency to suppose that people are polarized into two distinct groups: the lateral thinkers and the vertical thinkers. This is not a very useful polarization, since lateral and vertical thinking are complementary and are both parts of the thinking process. It is a matter of using both, not of choosing in which camp to settle. A more acceptable polarization is between those who see the need for lateral thinking and those who do not.

The negative creative temperament

The idea of a special creative temperament is a bit of a myth encouraged by those who feel that creativity is a special gift which deserves more recognition and consideration. The opposite temperament is, however, quite real. Negative creative temperament is strongly opposed to the idea of creativity. There is a rigid use of the YES/NO system. Everything has to be linked together in a clear, sequential process. Nothing can be considered unless it has developed directly from what has gone before. There is a total intolerance of ambiguity or of provocative ideas. In some cases this temperament is so extreme that it becomes an abnormal, psychiatric condition.

The creative temperament can always see several possibilities and is therefore difficult to convince of the unique validity of any particular approach. He is reluctant to make choices because a choice indicates too absolute a difference between the alternatives. He is unwilling to reject the other possibilities. The creative temperament is inclined to prefer uncommitted possibility and freedom of choice which remains free because choice is never made.

The negative creative temperament often can see only one possibility and is therefore convinced of its absolute rightness. To exclude the possibility of alternatives, he supports his single choice with logical buttressing because the correctness of this relieves him of the necessity for generating alternatives.

The negative creative temperament is intolerant of ambiguity, possibility, and what might happen next. The creative temperament finds all these things acceptable and useful.

Creativity as temperament

It may not be that creative people have a special temperament. It may be that a special temperament does give rise to creativity in a purely mechanical manner.
1. A dissatisfied person spends *more time* looking for change.
2. An egotist can carry a new idea *further* on his own.
3. Mistakes often provide a *creative jump*. A person who is careless might make the sort of mistake a methodical person would never make.
4. A person who is too lazy or too incompetent to do things in the accepted way has more chance of *finding a newer and easier way*.

These are all mechanical factors which favor creativity in the same way that a slow walker has more chance to notice things on a country walk.

Creativity as magic

This attitude is more often found in artists than in creative people in other fields. The belief is that creativity is a mystical quality and that any attempt to understand it will only ruin it, and any attempt to develop it is doomed to failure because it can only produce an analytical procedure. It is quite true that some artists may succeed in being creative only when a stewing anguish of emotions results in a powerful way of looking at things. But this is not the essence of creativity. Nor are such artists especially creative. The peculiarity of their personalities and emotional states does directly produce something which is new and unusual and, in that sense, there is a creative result.

Creativity in terms of escaping from old ideas and generating new ones is a function of the information handling system of the mind and not a matter of hobgoblins dancing around in the subconscious. Emotions and hobgoblins can introduce enough discontinuity to bring about creativity, but one does not have to rely on them in order to have discontinuity.

Creativity as lateral thinking

The creative temperament may be more inclined to introduce and use discontinuity than other temperaments. If nothing else is done, one may have to rely on this temperament (or chance) in order to have creativity. But if one can develop skill in introducing discontinuity and in using information creatively, then one no longer has to rely exclusively on natural temperament. The purpose of lateral thinking is to provide a process for using information in ways that bring about creative results. This makes creativity available to those who do not have creative temperaments. It is possible that so-called creative temperaments may find lateral thinking easier to understand and to use than other people. This happens with any tool. Those who understand its purpose and are interested in using it become more skilled in its use.

The dangers of creativity

16

Creativity is very necessary and very wonderful. In itself it should have no disadvantages since the business of creativity is to turn up useful ideas. And by definition useful ideas are not useless. In practice, however, there are dangers. These dangers arise from self-indulgence in creativity rather than from creativity itself.

● Creativity (and lateral thinking) brings about a change in direction. There is a change in the line of thinking, a change in the way something is looked at, a change in the way something is done. The purpose of a change is to provide a new direction. The change does not in itself provide any movement in the new direction. It is difficult to get anywhere if you are changing direction at every step. You cannot propel a boat very effectively just by flipping the rudder from one side to the other. Figure 16–1 suggests what happens if you change direction at every step. The lower part of the diagram shows how a change in direction is required only at intervals. And between the changes in direction one moves forward in a firm manner.

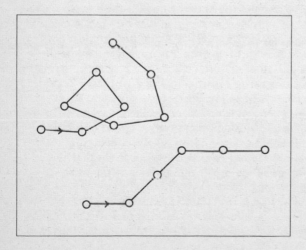

Figure 16–1.

Overindulgence in change for the sake of change can be very inefficient and costly. Change involves re-organization, re-tooling, re-stocking, and these are worthwhile only if one is going to work off the cost of the change before changing again. Change for the sake of change is to be encouraged in one's *thinking* in order to generate new ideas, but in *action* it becomes a danger.

● One idea breeds another and then another in a sort of chain reaction. The creative mind is attacked by all sorts of ideas; there are so many that the attractivenes of each one above the others lasts only for a short time. This can give rise to the "butterfly mind" effect, which means that an idea is pursued for a short time and then another, more interesting idea comes along and the first is dropped. The result is a litter of unfinished ideas, many of which might have been excellent if they had been carried through.

Another aspect of this loss of interest in an idea is the waste of completed ideas. A creative mind might get very interested in a problem or new device. But the interest is in the problem as a challenge. Once the problem is solved it is put aside and forgotten. The problem has served its purpose—which was to be solved. Once it has been solved, the usefulness of the solution is not of much importance to the creative person. This danger is easy to overcome if there is, working alongside the creative person, someone who is directly interested in the use of the solutions, and who uses them.

● The opposite of the butterfly mind is the obsessive urge to solve a problem or carry an idea through. A creative person may get so involved with a problem that he refuses to let it drop when it is no longer important. This pursuit of an idea for the sake of completion can be at the expense of other, more important ideas. It can happen that when circumstances change and a new product concept is no longer required, the creative person continues to work on that product for his own satisfaction in solving the problems involved. Interest in the problem itself has become more important than the usefulness of the problem in relation to the whole organization.

● Sheer interest in an idea acts as a powerful incentive to a creative person. This has two dangers. The first danger is that it is very difficult to get creative people interested in problems which do not interest them. The second danger is that a lot of time and money may be spent on pursuing ideas which are very interesting but are not nearly as important as other, less interesting ideas. Interest cannot easily be directed but arises naturally from the nature of the idea and not so much from the importance of that idea to someone else.

There is also the danger that an idea might be pursued as an idea. Thus, in the case of a technical problem, the researcher may pursue solutions which though scientifically fascinating are quite impractical in terms of the cost involved.

- A creative person develops a certain amount of pride in his ideas. This is especially so when he is not a very creative person. A very creative person has so many ideas that he cannot be too much concerned about any one of them. But a moderately creative person, or especially an uncreative person who has a single creative idea, becomes so involved in the idea that it becomes an extension of his ego. This means that the idea is defended and pursued at all costs even though it is obvious to everyone else that the idea, though a brilliant suggestion, is impractical.

- The sheer dynamism of a creative person may make him outrun his colleagues to the extent that they can have no controlling or moderating effect on his actions. This is especially so when the creative person has an executive ability as well. It is not that the creative person is unwilling to listen to others but that he is moving so far ahead that they cannot keep up with him. Although the ability to move ahead with ideas on one's own is the very essence of creativity, it can have its dangers in the business field. What usually happens is that the creative egotist moves ahead very fast and is successful but, because he is not open to adaptive influences (from his colleagues or the environment), he quickly reaches an impossible position and disaster follows. It is like the hound in a pack who moves so far ahead of his fellows that he is savaged by the stag. It is not so much a fault on the part of the creative person but a natural result of difference in speeds.

- Creative people usually work for their own satisfaction and to a slight extent for the purpose of impressing others with their creativity. The latter intention is much more marked in a group discussion situation, where there are others to be impressed. The danger, both with this personal satisfaction and also with the desire to impress others, is that the most creative, brilliant, ingenious, outlandish ideas tend to be favored at the expense of ordinary ideas. It is felt that ingenious solutions to a problem are much better than simple ones. Once again, the emphasis has shifted to the nature of the idea itself rather than to the use of that idea. As an artist, a creative person may become interested in the esthetics of his idea. He may tend to look down on the obvious idea which everyone could have had. In fact, if the obvious idea has come from someone who is not regarded for his creativity it will almost certainly be disregarded by the creative person.

The same thing happens when the original solution to a problem is obvious and humdrum. The creative people are then let loose on the problem. No matter what ideas they turn up, they will always be most reluctant to go back to the original solution and admit that they cannot find a better one.

● Just as the more creative ideas are valued and pursued at the expense of the more humdrum ideas, so creative people tend to undervalue a solid plodding person. Sometimes creative people tend to value creativity above effectiveness. This can really be dangerous if the creative people are concerned with running an organization. Creativity is more valuable than effectiveness only when it is added to effectiveness. In most fields, creativity by itself is worth much less than effectiveness. But creativity plus effectiveness is worth much more than effectiveness alone. In fact truly creative people do value the efficiency of the plodding, uncreative person—provided he builds a firm base under their creativity and is not always trying to knock it down.

● Creativity can be used as an excuse for inefficiency. It is claimed that a creative person cannot be bothered with detail. It is claimed that thoroughness is one thing and creativity is another and that it is a matter of deciding which is wanted but that both do not come together. Creative people are not necessarily as good at efficiency as they are at creativity. They may not even be as efficient as a person whose main virtue is efficiency. But there is no reason why creative persons should not have average efficiency. It is often not creative people who claim exemption from the rules of efficiency but the other way around. Inefficient people lay claim to creativity as a cover-up for their inefficiency.

- One of the dangers of creativity is that a lot of time may be wasted looking for the "ultimate" idea. Because creative people tend to be dissatisfied and tend to look beyond the adequate, they sometimes feel that there is an ultimate idea toward which they are groping. While they wait for this ultimate idea to be found they are disinclined to use ordinary but effective ideas. In the same way, a creative person shown an ordinary idea will always feel obliged to change it or improve it.

- Somewhat similar to looking for the ultimate idea is waiting for the breakthrough. A company may be in trouble but, instead of sitting down and working out quite ordinary methods of salvation, the managers just go on and hope that a wonderful creative breakthrough will come along and solve all their problems. The more trouble there is, the more emphasis there is on looking for the breakthrough that will mean salvation. Because a person is creative, he may tend to rely too much on this creativity to get him out of a difficulty.

- Creativity often involves an ability to tolerate ambiguity. It may sometimes be necessary to accept ambiguity in order to move forward to worthwhile ideas. This is a perfectly valid procedure, but it can be forgotten that the new idea rests at one point on this ambiguity. Ideally, once the idea has come about it should be checked out by working backward to establish a sound foundation for the idea. But this is sometimes overlooked if the idea seems good enough. Tolerance for ambiguity may be a necessary part of creativity but it has its own dangers for much may be hidden in this area of ambiguity (sometimes deliberately).

- Creativity involves the generation of alternatives. For a short space of time the creative effort (as in lateral thinking) is directed not toward solving the problem but toward generating alternative approaches. There is a slight danger that too great a success at generating alternatives may make it difficult to examine them all and to decide which is best. There may also be a reluctance to throw out an ingenious but impractical alternative. Creativity is often used as an excuse for indecisiveness.

Indecisiveness comes first and alternatives are quickly generated to explain it.

Many of the dangers listed above are not so much dangers of creativity but of the so-called creative temperament. When one has to rely on the creative temperament in order to get creativity, the above dangers are likely to occur. When one can add some skill in creativity to someone who is already aware of the need for effectiveness, the dangers are much less likely. That is one of the purposes of lateral thinking—to make creativity available as a skill which can be developed.

The other basis for the dangers is the usual tendency to polarize. It is felt that if one sees the point of creativity, one must be using it all the time and must value it above efficiency. The other extreme is to mistrust creativity and to feel that one can rely entirely on sound logic and experience. Both these extremes are ridiculous. But it is difficult to strike the right balance between the two. Creativity is not a fashionable gimmick, but neither is it a magic formula that will solve all problems.

Creativity is like the reverse shift in a car. You would not dream of driving along in reverse all the time. On the other hand, if you did not know how to use the reverse shift you would be unable to get out of blind alleys and your general maneuverability would be poor.

When one is aware of the dangers of creativity they cease to be so dangerous. One can watch for the danger signs in other people or in oneself. One can learn to use creativity as a tool instead of being dominated by it. Finally, one can avoid the self-indulgence that is not a real part of creativity at all.

Lateral thinking is a process that can be used

Lateral thinking is a way of using information in order to bring about creativity. A creative result may come about for several reasons, including chance stimulation or the unusual coming together of pieces of information. Lateral thinking is not the description of a *result* but a deliberate *way of thinking*. As such it can be used, whereas a result can only be admired.

Skill not chance, temperament, or gift

We tend to regard creativity as something brought about by chance, or as the byproduct of an ego-seeking temperament, or as a mysterious magic gift which some people have and others do not. Creativity is all these things, but only because we have made no attempt to introduce discontinuity into our thinking in any other way. That is why we have to rely on these factors for creativity. Creativity will continue to be associated with these factors, but not in an exclusive manner, once we have developed skill in lateral thinking. Such skill can be developed by anyone who takes the trouble to learn the principles and practice the process. Creativity need no longer be a matter of chance, temperament, or gift.

Patterning nature of mind

The need for lateral thinking arises from the nature of mind as a self-organizing information system. The characteristic of this broad class of systems is that they create patterns and use them. This is the basis of their great effectiveness. The fundamental feature of a patterning system is continuity. But in addition to establishing and using patterns, one needs from time to time to *break out* of them and put the available information together in a different way. This is absolutely necessary because a pattern depends not so much on the information it contains but on the arbitrary sequence in which that information arrived. Restructuring of patterns is not strongly developed in the mind and that is why humor and insight are so elusive. Lateral thinking is a way of using information in order to bring about the restructuring of patterns.

Escape from old ideas and generate new ones

The twin aspects of lateral thinking are the escape from old ideas and the generation of new ones. There does come a time when sheer pressure of events forces the restructuring of an old idea. But long before this enough information is available to allow the idea to be changed. By insight re-structuring, one can change an idea before being forced to.

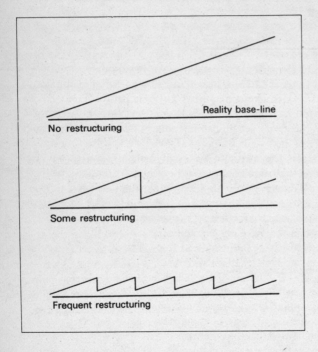

Figure 17–1.

Figure 17–1 shows the development of an idea as the reflection of "reality". ("Reality" is defined as that perception of events which gives the maximum effectiveness.) The idea diverges more and more from reality until pressure of events causes changes and the process starts again. If one can change ideas ahead of absolute necessity, then the process is as shown in the lowest part of the figure. Thus, one remains

220

close to reality all along. Restructuring is brought about by the escape from old ideas and the generation of new ones.

Lateral thinking is distinct from vertical thinking

The principles of lateral thinking are quite distinct from those of traditional, sequential, vertical thinking. Sometimes the principles are flatly contradictory. It is impossible to use lateral thinking unless one is quite clear about this distinction. For instance, in lateral thinking there may not be a reason for saying something until after it has been said. This provocative use of information is a basic principle of lateral thinking. Also in lateral thinking one may make use of an "intermediate impossible"; that is, a step which is quite unjustified on a logical, sequential basis but very useful as a stepping-stone to a new idea. The use of evaluation, judgment, and the NO function is quite different in lateral thinking. Lateral thinking seeks to find alternative ways of putting things together (lateral move) instead of looking for the best one and building on it (vertical move).

Lateral and vertical thinking are complementary

Lateral and vertical thinking are both required. Lateral thinking is concerned with the first stage of thinking, the stage of patterning, perceptual choice, and approach to the problem. Vertical thinking is concerned with second-stage processing and working out. Lateral thinking is concerned with choosing concepts, vertical thinking with using them. Lateral thinking requires vertical thinking to select and develop the ideas that are generated. Vertical thinking requires lateral thinking to establish an effective starting point. Skill in lateral thinking magnifies the effectiveness of skill in vertical thinking. And the other way around. Although the two types of thinking are distinct they are not substitutes; they are complementary.

Lateral thinking is practical

Lateral thinking is a practical way of using information and it can be learned, practiced, and used. The *first* stage is an understanding of the basis and necessity for lateral thinking. The *second* stage is developing an attitude of mind through familiarity with the principles. The *third* stage is the use of specific techniques, both to bring about creative results and also to develop the lateral thinking habit. In the *fourth* stage, lateral thinking has become a natural skill that can be used as and when required without recourse to the special techniques.

The new functional word PO

Just as the word NO is the functional basis of logical thinking so the word PO is the functional basis of lateral thinking. PO crystallizes the whole concept of lateral thinking into a tool for language and thought. If one understands PO one understands lateral thinking. Even if PO is not used in actual speech, it remains a symbol of the lateral thinking attitude toward the use of information and the creation of ideas. Once there is a practical tool such as PO, it becomes possible to use it and to develop a skill that can be transferred from one situation to another. It also becomes possible to introduce training in lateral thinking at an early stage in education.

Different aspects of creativity

Creativity is not concerned only with invention and new products. These are but a minor aspect of creativity. Creativity is concerned with the way information is looked at and the way it is used. Creativity comes into problem solving and into decision making. Creativity is as much the business of executive management as of R&D departments. Creativity is not just a matter of risking money on new products but also of saving money through avoiding the costly continuity of out-of-date ideas.

Creativity is not a luxury

There was a time when creativity was thought to be a luxury used mainly by artists. This has changed. Nowadays, creativity is seen to be an essential part of thinking. Creativity being the change of ideas is inseparable from the use of ideas. Since everyone uses ideas, creativity is everyone's business. Creativity is the process of change. This does not have to be a matter of huge, "bulk" change-overs, for it can be a matter of small changes at sensitive points with a gradual liberation from the restrictions of an old idea. Creativity does not only initiate change but it allows one to keep up with it. In a period of rapid change brought about by technology, education, communication, and developing attitudes one needs creativity more than ever. In a time of changing questions, shifting goals, and increasing complexity, one needs more than ever the ability to develop new ideas. As computers come to provide wonderful tools for information processing the emphasis is shifting back to the importance of ideas—the ideas that set the computer working, the ideas that make sense of the computer output.

Principles and use of lateral thinking

This book is not a collection of magic formulae to bring about creativity. Nor is it meant to be an inspirational book designed to sell the idea of creativity. The purpose of the book is to set out the *principles* and *use* of lateral thinking. Lateral thinking is not a "special" creativity gimmick but a fundamental way of thinking. There are various creativity techniques which have been developed and which make use of one or other of the basic principles of lateral thinking. Many people have used lateral thinking in the past. Many people are well aware of some of the principles involved. Lateral thinking is not a new magic, but a realization of the necessity for acknowledging this type of thinking as part of the thinking process. From this realization comes a need for formalization of the process so that those unacquainted with it can see what it is about, and those acquainted with it can find support for their way of thinking. This book is designed as a practical handbook for the development of skill in lateral thinking so that it may become a routine part of the thinking process.

Chapter Notes

need to introduce discontinuity in order to break out of established ideas and to provoke new ones.

MORE ABOUT PENGUINS, PELICANS AND PUFFINS

For further information about books available from Penguins please write to Dept EP, Penguin Books Ltd, Harmondsworth, Middlesex UB7 0DA.

In the U.S.A.: For a complete list of books available from Penguins in the United States write to Dept DG, Penguin Books, 299 Murray Hill Parkway, East Rutherford, New Jersey 07073.

In Canada: For a complete list of books available from Penguins in Canada write to Penguin Books Canada Ltd, 2801 John Street, Markham, Ontario L3R 1B4.

In Australia: For a complete list of books available from Penguins in Australia write to the Marketing Department, Penguin Books Australia Ltd, P.O. Box 257, Ringwood, Victoria 3134.

In New Zealand: For a complete list of books available from Penguins in New Zealand write to the Marketing Department, Penguin Books (N.Z.) Ltd, P.O. Box 4019, Auckland 10.

In India: For a complete list of books available from Penguins in India write to Penguin Overseas Ltd, 706 Eros Apartments, 56 Nehru Place, New Delhi 110019.

Edward de Bono

Opportunities
A Handbook of Business Opportunity Search

'An opportunity is as real an ingredient in business as raw material, labour or finance – but it only exists when you can see it'

Everybody assumes that he or she is opportunity-conscious but is frequently only conscious of the *need* to be opportunity-conscious. For often what looks like an opportunity isn't one after all.

Opportunities is a handbook which offers a total, systematic approach to opportunity-seeking at both corporate and executive levels. It is Edward de Bono's most significant contribution to business since he developed lateral thinking – and it should have just as much impact. Remember:

'Just before it comes into existence every business is an opportunity that someone has seen'

The Happiness Purpose

The proposed religion is based on the belief that the legitimate purpose of life is happiness and the best foundation for happiness is self-importance.

The happiness purpose is to be achieved through the use of thinking and humour and dignity. The ideal of love is to be replaced by the more reliable practice of respect.

The new religion may be used as a framework or as a philosophy. It may be used as a way of living or a way of looking at things. The new religion may be used on its own or in conjunction with any other religion.

Lucid, entertaining and provocative as always, Edward de Bono presents his blueprint for the disciplined pursuit of happiness which, in his opinion, is the legitimate purpose of life.

Edward de Bono

Wordpower

Could you make an *educated guess* at the *downside-risk* of a *marketing strategy*? Are you in the right *ball-game*, and faced with a crisis could you find an *ad hoc* solution?

These are just a few of the 265 specialized words – or 'thinking chunks' that Dr de Bono defines here in terms of their usage to help the reader use them as tools of expression. So the next time an economic adviser talks about cash-cows, or the local councillor starts a campaign about ecology, you know what to do. Reach for *Wordpower* and add a 'thinking chunk' to your vocabulary.

The Mechanism of Mind

Patterns made by drops of water on different surfaces or by electric bulbs in advertising displays help Dr de Bono, in this fascinating and provocative book, to build up a picture of a 'special memory-surface', which might resemble the brain in its selection, processing and rejection of information. With simple analogies he illustrates the mind's tendency to create and consolidate rigid patterns, to build myths, to polarize and divide, and then relates these mechanisms to the various modes of thinking – natural, logical, mathematical and lateral. In conclusion Edward de Bono coins and defines a new word of one syllable, with the startling suggestion that its addition to one language could greatly widen the effectiveness of human thinking.

Edward de Bono

Future Positive

Change by drift, change by protest, change by compromise; these are the moods of the sad seventies.

Edward de Bono writes here of the energetic eighties, of the positive future we can have if we want it. Societies, like organisms, develop certain characteristics that make further evolution impossible. At that point hallowed institutions and sacred ways of thinking have to be replaced with more positive ways. Our ancient negativity has to go.

There are no villains or stupid people and our troubles are due to the exercise of high intelligence within bubbles of limited perception. De Bono coins the term 'logic-bubbles' as a sort of mental notation. He also focuses attention on the all important 'edge-effect' and suggests that it may be difficult to journey North if we are never prepared to turn South.

Throughout the book Edward de Bono is not afraid to be provocative, for as he says, 'provocation is as important for creativity as analysis is for truth.' Some ideas he suggests are meant to be taken seriously but others are meant only as provocations. He has no time for the CYA attitude – which suggests that you are unable to do anything positive because you forever hold your hands in such a position as to minimize the effect of a kick in the pants.

Also published in Pelicans

THE FIVE-DAY COURSE IN THINKING
LATERAL THINKING
PO: BEYOND YES AND NO
PRACTICAL THINKING: Four Ways to be Right: Five Ways to be Wrong: Five Ways to Understand
TEACHING THINKING
THE USE OF LATERAL THINKING

An Insight into Management Accounting
John Sizer

During the last decade managements have had to learn to live with high rates of inflation, low levels of profitability, and serious liquidity problems. The more sophisticated techniques developed by management accountants in response to these conditions are described in the second edition of Professor Sizer's best-selling work. It has been extensively revised and extended by almost two hundred pages.

'For managers and management students rather than professional accountants. The author explains the elements of financial and cost accounting and goes on to consider financial planning, investment appraisal, budgetary control and decision making. This is no easy popularisation but a substantial contribution to an important subject' – *The Times Educational Supplement*

The Multinationals
Christopher Tugendhat

In recent years vast international companies have developed which dominate the 'commanding heights of the economy' throughout Western Europe and North America. Firms like Alcan, IBM, Ford, Shell and Bayer have annual sales as large as the gross national products of many countries, and their rate of growth is much faster. Inevitably there are tensions between the companies and governments who see control of a vital sector of the economy slipping from their grasp.

Christopher Tugendhat's book, which won a McKinsey Foundation Book Award in 1971, is a detailed examination of the multinationals and the political implications of their position and influence. His theories and principles, supported with examples from the experience of companies and governments, illuminate a major political and economic problem.

'The importance of this book is not in doubt. It will stand the test of years' – Tam Dalyell in the *New Scientist*

The Penguin Dictionary of Commerce
Michael Greener

Specially designed to resolve the increasing complexity of business life for the ordinary person, this dictionary answers hundreds of queries on all aspects of commerce and gives the literal meaning, the usage and the limitations of those commercial terms which interest the layman as businessman, taxpayer and investor.

The Penguin Dictionary of Computers
Antony Chandor, with John Graham and Robin Williamson

A glossary of some 3,000 words, phrases and acronyms used in connection with computers. It has been designed both to assist technical readers and the increasing number of non-specialists whose work is to some extent affected by computers. In addition there are 70 general articles in the major computer topics and such business processes as 'budgetary control' and 'systems analysis' which are increasingly being handled by computers.

The Galbraith Reader
J. K. Galbraith

Here is the best of his writing, including selections from *The Affluent Society*, *The Great Crash*, *The New Industrial State* and *Money*; together with more personal items, excerpts from his *Ambassador's Journal*, and letters to President Kennedy describing a nation and a world moving towards crisis. Here is a glittering prose mosaic of the Galbraith style, a portrait of a great man forever challenging the beliefs of his generation.

'A singular delight . . . the delight of consistent good prose, and of a thinking man thinking' – *The New York Times*

Organization Theory

Edited by D. S. Pugh

The editor of this volume of Readings defines organization theory as 'the study of the structure, functions and performance of organizations and the behaviour of groups and individuals within them'.

From the point of view of organizational behaviour, the task of management can be considered as the organization of individuals in relation to the physical means and resources to achieve the desired goal. In Part One the continuing activities of task allocation, coordination and supervision, which constitute the organization's structure, are discussed. A theoretical analysis of what managers have to do is given in Part Two. Part Three describes behaviour in organizations. Included here is a section of Elton Mayo's key Hawthorne studies – the human relations approach. Some of the research by Lewin on group dynamics, attitude change and leadership style is also examined.

Management and Motivation

Edited by Victor H. Vroom and Edward L. Deci

The performance of anyone at his job is affected by a combination of ability and motivation. This book brings together papers which represent the main work being done in the study of motivation.

There are three main approaches to the subject. The first is paternalistic in nature and assumes that the more a worker is rewarded, the harder he will work. The second approach assumes that a person will be motivated to work if rewards and penalties are tied directly to his performance. The third approach is that called participative management in which the incentives for effective performance are in the job itself or in the individual's relationship with members of his working team.